Trichotillomania

Trichotillomania

AN ACT-ENHANCED BEHAVIOR THERAPY APPROACH

Therapist Guide

Douglas W. Woods • Michael P. Twohig

OXFORD
UNIVERSITY PRESS

2008

OXFORD
UNIVERSITY PRESS

Oxford University Press, Inc., publishes works that further
Oxford University's objective of excellence
in research, scholarship, and education.

Oxford   New York
Auckland   Cape Town   Dar es Salaam   Hong Kong   Karachi
Kuala Lumpur   Madrid   Melbourne   Mexico City   Nairobi
New Delhi   Shanghai   Taipei   Toronto

With offices in
Argentina   Austria   Brazil   Chile   Czech Republic   France   Greece
Guatemala   Hungary   Italy   Japan   Poland   Portugal   Singapore
South Korea   Switzerland   Thailand   Turkey   Ukraine   Vietnam

Published by Oxford University Press, Inc.
198 Madison Avenue, New York, New York 10016

www.oup.com

Library of Congress Cataloging-in-Publication Data
Woods, Douglas W., 1971–
Trichotillomania : an ACT-enhanced behavior therapy approach : therapist
guide / Douglas W. Woods, Michael P. Twohig.
p. ; cm. — (TreatmentsThatWork)
Includes bibliographical references.
ISBN 978-0-19-533603-0
1. Compulsive hair pulling—Treatment.   2. Acceptance and
commitment therapy.   3. Behavior therapy.
[DNLM: 1. Trichotillomania—psychology.   2. Trichotillomania—
therapy.   3. Behavior Therapy—methods.   4. Models, Psychological.
WM 190 W894t 2008]   I. Twohig, Michael P   II. Title.   III.
Treatments that work.
RC569.5.H34W66 2008
616.85′8406—dc22   2007035120

9 8 7 6 5 4 3 2 1

Printed in the United States of America
on acid-free paper

About Treatments *ThatWork*™

While stunning developments have taken place in health care over the last several years, many of our widely accepted interventions and strategies in mental health and behavioral medicine have been brought into question by research evidence as not only lacking benefit but, perhaps, inducing harm. Other strategies have been proven effective through use of the best current standards of evidence, resulting in broad-based recommendations to make these practices more available to the public. Several recent developments are behind this revolution. First, we have arrived at a much deeper understanding of pathology, both psychological and physical, which has led to the creation of new, more precisely targeted interventions. Second, our research methodologies have improved substantially, such that we have reduced threats to internal and external validity, making the outcomes more directly applicable to clinical situations. Third, governments around the world and health care systems and policy makers have decided that the quality of care should improve, that it should be evidence based, and that it is in the public's interest to ensure that this improvement happens (Barlow, 2004; Institute of Medicine, 2001).

Of course, the major stumbling block for clinicians everywhere is the accessibility of newly developed evidence-based psychological interventions. Workshops and books can go only so far in acquainting responsible and conscientious practitioners with the latest behavioral health care practices and their applicability to individual patients. This new series, Treatments *ThatWork*™, is devoted to communicating these exciting new interventions to clinicians on the frontlines of practice. The manuals and workbooks in this series contain step-by-step detailed procedures for assessing and treating specific problems and diagnoses. This series also goes beyond the books and manuals by providing ancillary materials that will approximate the supervisory process in assisting practitioners in the implementation of these procedures in their practice.

In our emerging health care system, the growing consensus is that evidence-based practice offers the most responsible course of action for the mental health professional. All behavioral health care clinicians deeply desire to provide the best possible care for their patients. In this series, our aim is to close the dissemination and information gap and make that care possible.

This therapist guide, and the companion workbook for clients, addresses the treatment of trichotillomania (TTM), a disorder in which individuals engage in the repetitive pulling of their hair to the point of noticeable hair loss and functional impairment. The treatment approach described blends traditional behavior therapy elements of habit reversal training and stimulus control techniques with the more contemporary behavioral elements of acceptance and commitment therapy (ACT). Unlike typical interventions that focus on helping clients change their negative thinking to reduce the urge to pull, the goal of this treatment is to get clients to accept their urges without fighting against them. Over 10 weeks, clients learn to recognize their pulling and the events or situations that lead them to pull, ways of stopping or preventing pulling, and how to accept the uncontrollable internal experiences that cause them to pull. This guide comes complete with step-by-step instructions for every session, as well as metaphors, exercises, and home assignments to facilitate therapy and ensure success. Designed to be used with older adolescents and adults, this innovative intervention has proven efficacy and is sure to be a powerful tool for the clinician who treats TTM.

David H. Barlow, Editor-in-Chief,
Programs *That Work*™
Boston, Massachusetts

References

Barlow, D. H. (2004). Psychological treatments. *American Psychologist, 59,* 869–878.

Institute of Medicine (2001). *Crossing the quality chasm: A new health system for the 21st century.* Washington, DC: National Academy Press.

Contents

Chapter 1 | *Introductory Information for Therapists*

Background Information and Purpose of This Program

Trichotillomania (TTM) is a disorder of secrecy and shame. Many who have it do not know it has a name, and many who know what they have cannot find treatment providers who know what it is. Indeed, research on the etiology, maintenance, and treatment of TTM is limited. As a result, few effective therapeutic options exist. Behavior therapy has the greatest empirical support, having reliably outperformed medications in head-to-head, albeit small, efficacy trials. Unfortunately, the number of mental health providers familiar with TTM and its treatment is quite small. This manual was written as a tool for therapists to become familiar with an effective treatment for TTM.

Acceptance and Commitment Therapy (ACT) Enhanced Behavior Therapy for Trichotillomania (AEBT-T) is a 10-session treatment package for older adolescents and adults. The treatment blends traditional behavior therapy elements of habit reversal training and stimulus control (HRT/SC) techniques (Woods & Miltenberger, 1995) with the more contemporary behavioral elements of ACT (Hayes, Strosahl, & Wilson 1999). The goal of this program is twofold: to reduce hair pulling and actively increase the client's quality of life.

Trichotillomania

This disorder involves the repetitive pulling of one's hair to the point of noticeable hair loss and functional impairment. The *Diagnostic and Statistical Manual of Mental Disorders* (fourth edition, text revision; *DSM-IV-TR*; American Psychiatric Association, 2000) criteria also include tension prior to pulling or when attempting to resist pulling, and subsequent relief of this tension following pulling. There is considerable debate as to the utility of the latter two criteria. Using the *DSM-IV-TR* criteria, which include tension and subsequent reduction, the prevalence of TTM is approximately 0.6% (Christenson, Pyle, & Mitchell, 1991). However, when the criteria of tension and tension reduction are excluded, prevalence is approximately 3% (Christenson, Pyle, & Mitchell, 1991). Trichotillomania is more common in women, with estimates of female-to-male ratios being in the 3–9:1 range (Christenson, Mackenzie, & Mitchell, 1994). For this reason, the text of this manual incorporates the use of female pronouns throughout. TTM also follows a chronic waxing and waning course (Stein, Christenson, & Hollander, 1999), and the average age of onset is 13 years (Mansueto, Townsley-Stemberger, Thomas, & Golomb, 1997).

Impairment Associated with Trichotillomania

Along with the requisite hair loss, TTM can produce a variety of physical difficulties. Approximately 48%–77% of individuals place the pulled hair in or around their mouth and 5%–18% of individuals ingest it (Christenson & Mansueto, 1999), which occasionally results in the formation of trichobezoars (conglomerates of hair and food that form in the gastrointestinal tract). Trichobezoars may result in a failure to gain weight or in weight loss, iron deficiency anemia, pain, vomiting, fever, distension, halitosis, hyperproteinemia (abnormally high levels of protein in the blood), and steatorrhea (excessive excretion of fecal fat). In some cases, surgical removal of the trichobezoar may be required (Phillips, Zaheer, & Drugas, 1998). Other medical complications can include scalp irritation, follicle damage, atypical regrowth of hair, dental damage such as gum disease and enamel erosion from hair mouthing, finger calluses, muscle fatigue, and carpal tunnel syndrome (Keuthen, Stein, & Christenson, 2001).

Trichotillomania may also produce significant psychosocial impairment. Recently, a collaborative research group formed by the Trichotillomania Learning Center completed the largest study ever done on the impact of TTM in adults (Woods, Flessner, et al., 2006a). A total of 1,697 individuals with chronic hair-pulling were surveyed across numerous domains of functioning. In this study, 55.8% reported pulling during 30% or more of their day. Likewise, 70% felt that TTM had led to the development of additional psychiatric disorders, and as a whole, the sample group experienced clinically elevated levels of depressive, anxious, and stress symptoms, which were similar in magnitude to those found in samples of persons with obsessive-compulsive disorder (OCD; Antony, Bieling, Cox, Enns, & Swinson, 1998).

Trichotillomania appears to be associated with high psychiatric comorbidity, as 35%–55% of individuals with TTM have a lifetime history of major depression, 50%–57% have a history of anxiety disorders, 22%–35% have a history of substance use disorders, and approximately 20% have experienced eating disorders (Christenson, Mackenzie, & Mitchell, 1991; Christenson & Mackenzie, 1994). In sum, up to 82% of individuals with TTM currently meet or have met criteria for a comorbid Axis I diagnosis (Christenson, Mackenzie, & Mitchell, 1991).

Individuals with TTM are also likely to experience a host of social, academic, occupational, and financial difficulties. They frequently avoid routine activities such as swimming, going to the hairdresser, and going outside on windy days (Woods, Flessner, et al., 2006a). In severe cases, individuals with visible hair loss may avoid intimate and social relationships or certain occupations where hair loss is likely to be noticed, and they may contemplate suicide (Seedat & Stein, 1998; Woods, Flessner et al., 2006a). Individuals with TTM also report a moderate negative impact on academic performance, with 76% reporting that pulling has caused difficulties in studying (Woods, Flessner, et al., 2006a). Limited data exist on the occupational impact of TTM, but a survey of 58 persons with the disorder found that 55% reported occupational impairment as a direct result of the pulling (Keuthen et al., 2002). Estimates are that nearly one million work days are missed per year due to TTM symptoms, and nearly 73,000 working-age adults may have ended their employment because of TTM (Woods, Flessner, et al., 2006a). Finally, individuals with TTM are often affected financially by trying to mask the effects of the disorder through purchases such as makeup to cover damaged areas.

Diagnostic Criteria for Trichotillomania

In Table 1.1 we list the *DSM-IV-TR* criteria for trichotillomania.

Behavioral Model of Trichotillomania

Mansueto and colleagues (1997) offered the first comprehensive model for TTM, which encouraged clinicians to understand the multiple levels and sources of influence that could maintain pulling in those with the disorder. Mansueto's model has had a profound impact on how TTM is understood and treated. Until the Mansueto model was offered, treatment focused primarily on habit reversal training. With the emergence of the Mansueto model, therapeutic attention began to incorporate interventions to prevent pulling episodes from occurring (i.e., stimulus control) and highlighted the importance of focusing on interventions to deal with the private experiences that often give rise to pulling (e.g., urges, cravings, cognitions).

In the following sections, we broadly review the types of variables Mansueto and colleagues implicated in the original comprehensive model of TTM. In addition, we discuss new findings that have helped to shape our own emerging model (Wetterneck & Woods, 2007). The most striking difference between the original model and our emerging model in-

Table 1.1 *DSM-IV-TR* Criteria for Trichotillomania

Each of the following criteria must be met to qualify for a diagnosis of TTM:

A. Recurrent pulling out of one's hair resulting in noticeable hair loss

B. An increasing sense of tension immediately before pulling out the hair or when attempting to resist the behavior

C. Pleasure, gratification, or relief when pulling out the hair

D. The disturbance is not better accounted for by another mental disorder and is not due to a general medical condition.

E. The disturbance causes clinically significant distress or impairment in social, occupational, or other important areas of functioning.

Source: The *Diagnostic and Statistical Manual of Mental Disorders* (fourth edition, text revision), American Psychiatric Association (2000).

volves the functional role of private events (e.g., cognitions, urges, cravings, emotions) in the maintenance of pulling. We agree with Mansueto et al. that these variables likely influence pulling, however, there is some discrepancy in the target of intervention. Traditional cognitive-behavioral therapy (CBT) methods, which stem from Mansueto's model, have focused primarily on reducing or otherwise altering the private experiences in the service of pulling reduction. Such therapy focuses on more accurate thinking, learning to relax, or figuring out new ways to reduce the urge. Recent research suggests, however, that it is not simply the urges, cravings, cognitions, and emotions that may be responsible for some episodes of pulling, but rather the larger context that the client brings to the table. If the client has a general tendency to avoid, reduce, or escape from unwanted private experiences (a pattern called "experiential avoidance"), it is only then that the private experiences exert influence over pulling. As a result, the current treatment de-emphasizes attempts to modify or eliminate private experiences and focuses instead on acceptance of such phenomena.

The various factors that have been implicated in the maintenance of pulling are described in the sections that follow. These factors include antecedent triggers and reinforcing consequences, which can be environmental, emotional, and/or cognitive.

Environmental Triggers Associated with Pulling

A number of environmental factors have been associated with increased TTM symptoms including different *settings or activities*. For example, pulling commonly occurs in one's bedroom and/or bathroom and is likely to increase with sedentary activities such as driving, reading, and watching television (Mansueto et al., 1997). Specific *physical, visual,* and *tactile stimuli* also frequently bring on pulling. For example, hair pullers often seek out target hairs that possess specific physical qualities such as a certain color, shape, or texture. Stein and colleagues (1999) noted that coarse, thick, wiry, or stubbly hairs are often pulled. Various *environmental changes following pulling* contribute to TTM by reinforcing the pulling. For example, specific tangible features of the hair may actually reinforce pulling or pre-pulling behaviors (e.g., the tactile stimulation achieved from stroking hair or otherwise twisting hair; Mansueto et al., 1997; Rapp et al., 2000). The pulled hair may be rubbed against a person's body, often the face or between fingers, or certain types of hairs (e.g., coarse hair or those with plump roots) may be more appealing to the puller. People with TTM often spend more time manipulating hair than actually pulling hair (Miltenberger, Long,, Rapp, Lumley, & Elliott, 1998).

Emotional Factors Associated with Pulling

Although TTM is not a mood or anxiety disorder, various emotional states may evoke pulling. Research has focused primarily on the evocative effects of states such as anxiety, tension, and boredom, but has also implicated emotional states such as loneliness, fatigue, guilt, anger, indecision, frustration, and excitement (Mansueto et al., 1997). In addition, those with TTM often report that prior to their pulling, they experience bodily sensations (i.e., general tension, sensations localized to specific areas) or general discomfort (i.e., vague urges, inner pressure, or feeling not "just right") before many of their pulling episodes (Wetterneck, Woods, Flessner, Norberg, & Begotka, 2005). Phenomenological studies on those with TTM suggest that pulling often results in a temporary reduction of these unpleasant emotional states.

Interestingly, there is growing evidence that the relationship between specific emotional states and TTM severity may be moderated by an individual's history of escaping or avoiding unpleasant emotions or cognitions. This variable, experiential avoidance (Hayes, Wilson, Gifford, Follette, & Strosahl, 1996), may be particularly important in the analysis of TTM according to a study by Begotka, Woods, and Wetterneck (2004), who showed a significant relationship between pulling severity (as measured by the Massachusetts General Hospital Hairpulling Scale [MGH-HS]; Keuthen et al., 1995) and experiential avoidance (as measured by the Acceptance and Action Questionnaire [AAQ]; Hayes et al., 2004). With respect to the relationship between various emotional states and pulling severity, it was found that worry and physiological arousal symptoms prior to pulling were significantly correlated with higher TTM severity, a relationship moderated by experiential avoidance (Wetterneck & Woods, 2005). In other words, the more someone attempts to avoid or control unpleasant private experiences in general, the more likely they are to pull in reaction to an urge or negative emotion.

Cognitive Factors Associated with Pulling

Specific cognitions may also come to occasion pulling. For example, seeing a coarse or gray hair in the mirror may evoke thoughts that lead to the removal of the hair (e.g., "My eyebrows should be symmetrical" or "Gray hairs are bad, and I need to remove them"). In addition, those with more dysfunctional beliefs about their appearance, greater thoughts of shame, and fears about being evaluated negatively, experience more severe TTM (Norberg, Wetterneck, Woods, & Conelea, 2007). However, as with the relationships between TTM severity and specific emotional states, these relationships diminish or disappear when controlling for experiential avoidance. Taken together, these results suggest that components of TTM treatment targeting the cognitive or emotional factors contributing to pulling should consider addressing the individual's general tendency to escape from or avoid these events.

In sum, research has shown that thoughts and feelings (including urges to pull) play a meaningful role in the development and maintenance of TTM. These findings also suggest that it is not the mere presence of these cognitive variables that predicts greater TTM severity but the way in which one generally interacts with and responds to these events. The process of fighting against, controlling, and otherwise attempting to avoid or escape one's thoughts about or urges to pull might be an important variable to address in the treatment of TTM. Thus, from our perspective, treatment should focus on decreasing the influence these events have on pulling by decreasing the client's efforts to control them. For this reason, we have incorporated an acceptance-based procedure, ACT, as it focuses on teaching people how to reduce the influence of, and their own fight against, their private events.

Evidence for Different Processes Underlying Pulling

Mounting evidence suggests that there are at least two unique processes underlying pulling in TTM. *Focused pulling* is preceded by a private internal event such as an urge, bodily sensation (e.g., itching or burning), emotion (e.g., anxiety), or cognition (e.g., "I can't stand this any longer"). It is believed that focused pulling occurs as a specific behavior designed to temporarily reduce or escape from these experiences or to intentionally acquire a short-term pleasurable sensation that is sometimes experienced by those with TTM (Grant, Odlaug, & Potenza, 2007). In contrast, *automatic pulling* seems to occur outside of one's awareness, often during sedentary activities (e.g., watching television, reading, or driving) and without any identifiable private antecedent. It is commonly believed that many individuals with TTM experience both processes, and it can often be difficult to tell, in any one episode of pulling, which process is active. For this reason, although AEBT-T includes different interventions for these two processes, it is important that both interventions be used in the proscribed manner.

Empirical confirmation of the focused and automatic distinction is growing. Researchers have found that many individuals with TTM are likely to report decreases in anxiety and tension following episodes of pulling (Diefenbach, Mouton-Odum, & Stanley, 2002). Another recent study found that in 47 patients with TTM, 34% characterized their pulling as primarily "focused," 47% as primarily "automatic," and 19% as equally focused and automatic (du Toit, van Kradenburg, Niehaus, & Stein, 2001). One of the largest limitations in validating the focused–automatic distinction has been the lack of a standard measure to assess the construct. Recently, the research group at the University of Wisconsin-Milwaukee created the Milwaukee Inventory for Subtypes of Trichotillomania–Adult (MIST-A) to formally assess these pulling subtypes (Flessner et al., in press). Not only did the emergent factor structure support the distinction between focused and automatic pulling, but as predicted, the validity data from the study were consistent with the purported habitual versus emotion regulation functions. For example, scores on the Automatic scale of the MIST-A were negatively related to the participants' self-reported level of awareness, demonstrating that the more automatic the person's pulling, the less aware they were of their pulling episodes. Likewise, correlations between the Automatic scale and the Depression, Anxiety, and Stress subscales of the short-form version of the Depression Anxiety Stress Scales (DASS-21) (Lovibond & Lovibond, 1995) were very weak. In contrast, scores on the Focused scale were significantly and moderately correlated with the DASS-21 Depression, Anxiety, and Stress subscales (Flessner et al., in press).

Research also suggests that the different pulling processes are differentially related to experiential avoidance. Self-reported levels of focused, but not automatic, pulling were significantly positively correlated with experiential avoidance (Begotka, Woods, & Wetterneck, 2003). In another study, those with primarily focused pulling, primarily automatic pulling, and mixed focused and automatic pulling were compared on the DASS-21 subscales after controlling for TTM severity (Flessner et al., in press). Results suggested that those individuals with primarily automatic pulling experienced less depressive, anxiety, and stress symptoms than those with primarily focused or mixed patterns. Likewise, those with mixed pulling experienced more depressive, anxious, and stress symptoms than those with either primarily focused or automatic pulling.

Development of This Treatment Program and Evidence Base

The AEBT-T manual was developed for therapists treating adults with TTM, though it could likely be extended to individuals in mid- to late adolescence. The manual was intended for therapists who are familiar with behavior therapy and who have familiarized themselves with acceptance- or mindfulness-based treatments. In addition, as the manual was developed, it was expected that therapists implementing the treatment would already possess and integrate into the manual an exceptional set of broad therapeutic skills (e.g., empathy, summarization, reflective listening, etc.).

Originally this manual was developed on the behavioral model of TTM just discussed, which defines TTM as involving two core behavioral processes: automatic and focused pulling. Given these two processes, the first version of this manual used HRT/SC procedures to treat automatic pulling, and ACT to treat focused pulling via reduction of experiential avoidance and an engagement in valued living.

The original manual was evaluated and revised through an empirical process. In the initial feasibility trial of AEBT-T (Twohig & Woods, 2004), a seven-session treatment manual was used for six adults with TTM. Of the six participants, one had comorbid anxiety disorders, one had comorbid mood disorders, and two were on psychotropic medications. The study had a multiple baseline across subjects design, and the treatment was delivered in weekly individual sessions. The first five sessions were 1 hour in duration and the final two each lasted 30 minutes. During the four ACT-focused sessions, treatment centered on (a) abandoning strategies used to control urges to pull, thoughts, emotions, or other aversive private experiences, (b) acceptance of or willingness to experience one's pulling-related private events, (c) defusion from the literal meaning of language, and (d) reorienting thoughts toward increasing quality of life or heading in a valued-life direction. Habit reversal training was implemented in the fifth session and reviewed in Sessions 6 and 7. These sessions occurred during the 3 weeks following the ACT-only sessions. The HRT was used to help the participant become aware of her pulling, teach an incompatible behavior to replace pulling, and get the assistance of a peer to maintain use of the procedure.

Self-reports of pulling showed that the intervention resulted in decreases to zero levels of pulling for four of the six subjects, and the results were maintained for three of the four subjects at 3-month follow-up. Moderate decreases were seen in pulling of the remaining two subjects. The MGH-HS scores collected at pretreatment, post-treatment, and follow-up showed a 63% reduction at post-treatment, with gains maintained at follow-up. Independent photograph ratings confirmed the self-report findings, and all subjects evaluated the treatment positively.

Based on the feasibility trial, the manual was revised to increase the number of sessions from 7 to 10, reorganize the order of the ACT components, and incorporate relapse prevention techniques. The modified manual was then tested in a small randomized, clinical trial funded by the Trichotillomania Learning Center (TLC; www.trich.org), a national patient advocacy organization for individuals with TTM and related body-focused repetitive behaviors. Twenty-eight participants were randomly assigned to one of the two conditions (14 AEBT-T, and 14 waitlist [WL] control). Two people from the AEBT-T group and one person from the WL condition dropped out for reasons unrelated to the study. A blinded independent evaluator (IE) conducted assessments pre- and post-treatment. At the end of the post-treatment assessment, the WL participants were offered AEBT-T and reassessed at the end of treatment. All individuals in the initial AEBT-T condition were reassessed at a 3-month follow-up. In addition to assessing pulling severity with the

MGH-HS and IE ratings (NIMH-TIS Rating), depression and anxiety measures were taken, as was a measure of experiential avoidance.

Results showed that pulling severity across the two primary outcome measures (i.e., pulling severity and related impairment) decreased for the AEBT-T group, but not for the WL group (between-group differences: dMGH $= 1.71$, dNIMH-Impairment $= 1.38$). Likewise, after the WL group received AEBT-T, they also showed significant decreases in all indicators of pulling severity. Overall, 66% of AEBT-T recipients were deemed "treatment responders," and significant differences were maintained at the 3-month follow-up on the MGH-HS. In addition to the gains seen in hair-pulling symptoms, depression and anxiety scores also decreased for the AEBT-T group but not for the WL group (Woods, Wetterneck, & Flessner, 2006).

Additional analyses of potential mechanisms of change indicated that pre–post decreases in an experiential avoidance measure (as measured by the Acceptance and Action Questionnaire [AAQ]) were moderately and significantly correlated with pre–post decreases in pulling severity ($r = .59$). Subject compliance ratings completed by both clinician and participant were also positively and significantly correlated with reduction of symptoms at post-treatment ($r = .57–.67$).

The Role of Medications

The most common intervention for TTM is pharmacotherapy (Woods, Flessner, et al., 2006b) despite the fact that evidence supporting this strategy is quite limited. To date, only six randomized controlled trials (RCTs) evaluating the efficacy of pharmacotherapy have been conducted. Typically, selective serotonin reuptake inhibitors (SSRIs) are the treatment of choice (Woods, Flessner, et al., 2006b), but only one study (Swedo et al., 1989) has demonstrated the superiority of medications (i.e., clomipramine) over another medication or placebo. In the two RCTs comparing behavior therapy to SSRIs, behavior therapy outperformed the medications (Ninan, Rothbaum, Martsteller, Knight, & Eccard, 2000; van Minnen, Hoogduin, Keijsers, Hellenbrand, & Hendriks, 2003). Despite the failure of medications to reduce TTM symptoms, they may be helpful in managing the disorders developing secondary to

TTM, such as depression or social phobia, or for those disorders that co-occur with TTM and can exacerbate TTM symptoms (e.g., anxiety).

Overview of AEBT-T

Acceptance and Commitment Therapy Enhanced Behavior Therapy for Trichotillomania (AEBT-T) is a combination of habit reversal training (HRT) and stimulus control (SC) procedures as well as acceptance and commitment therapy (ACT). Selection of these treatment elements was guided by the behavioral model of TTM described earlier. Both HRT/SC and ACT are behavior therapies based on the principles of operant learning theory, which describes how environmental antecedents and consequences can interact with a particular biological makeup to cause and maintain certain patterns of responding. Acceptance and commitment therapy is further informed by relational frame theory (Hayes, Barnes-Holmes, & Roche, 2001), a behavior analytic account of language and cognition that attempts to explain how internal private experiences influence traditional behavioral processes.

The purpose of the treatment is to educate the client about TTM and teach her to (a) be aware of her pulling and its antecedents, (b) use self-management strategies to prevent or stop the pulling, (c) stop fighting against private experiences that lead to pulling, through learning skills such as defusion and acceptance, and (d) work consistently toward increasing her quality of life.

Elements of HRT and SC are incorporated, as they are believed to be effective in treating automatic pulling. HRT/SC procedures focus on bringing the pulling into awareness and then providing and reinforcing the use of strategies to prevent the pulling or to make it more difficult. ACT procedures focus on teaching the client skills to step out of the struggle with urges to pull. The goal of ACT more specifically is not to try to alter these private experiences, nor do ACT therapists suggest or even imply that an accepting stance toward these stimuli will ultimately result in their reduction. Rather, the therapist creates a therapeutic context through the use of metaphors and experiential exercises that supports viewing urges, thoughts, or feelings as stimuli to be observed, rather than acted on. Clients learn that when such stimuli are present, they are present. When they are absent, they are absent. When they are weak, they are weak, and when they are strong, they are strong. The clinician works to allow the client to see that she has a choice to either (a) experience the private events and refrain from pulling while engaging in more meaningful activities or (b) fight with her private events, pull to control them, and, as a result, be taken away from areas of life that are really important to her. Following is a brief overview of treatment sessions.

Session 1. The therapist provides an overview of AEBT-T, psychoeducation about TTM, a review of situations likely to exacerbate pulling, an introduction to the self-monitoring homework assignments, and a discussion of therapeutic expectations.

Session 2. This session includes the implementation of SC strategies and HRT.

Session 3. During this session, the therapist and client begin to identify what is important to the client and ways in which the struggle with urges to pull has interfered with her quality of life.

Session 4. In this session discussion of perceived barriers to pursuing better quality of life continues. These barriers stem from attempts to control unwanted private experiences. After identifying strategies the client uses to control her urges to pull as well as her emotions, thoughts, and feelings surrounding the pulling, the therapist and client discuss the effectiveness of current strategies. The goal of the session is to demonstrate the ultimate ineffectiveness of and problematic results stemming from attempts to control urges, emotions, thoughts, and feelings.

Session 5. This session is a continuation of the topics discussed in Session 4. Additional time is spent on how someone can fall into the trap of trying to control urges to pull hair. Through experiential exercises and the use of metaphors, the client can experience the difficulty involved in suppressing or controlling private events. Alternative ways (other than pulling) of responding to private events are discussed. After relating this difficulty to the client's attempts at controlling private experience through pulling, she is asked to consider the possibility of experiencing willingness to accept private events, as a potentially alternative response. The session ends with an introduction to making "behavioral commitments" as an opportunity to practice willingness in the service of valued living.

Behavioral commitments will continue to be stressed throughout the course of therapy.

Sessions 6 and 7. In these sessions the client begins to learn that one can experience the private events as observable responses rather than as literal objects or truth. This process is called "cognitive defusion."

Session 8. In this session the client has an opportunity to practice the material presented in previous sessions. The client is also encouraged to embrace the urge by being exposed to various cues that are likely to trigger the urge to pull.

Session 9. The client is again given the opportunity to practice the techniques learned in therapy, and material covered in therapy to date is reviewed.

Session 10. Here the processes needed for each client are determined. This assessment may involve a review of values, acceptance, and defusion, as well as of the HRT and SC procedures. This final session also involves the implementation of relapse prevention procedures, including discussions on lapse versus relapse, vigilance with HRT and SC procedures, and the return of fusion and cognitive or emotional control.

It is important to note that while AEBT-T was originally designed as a 10-session treatment, you should use your data-guided clinical judgment to determine how rapidly to progress through therapy and when termination is appropriate. Also, you should consider the possibility that periodic booster sessions may be required for maintenance of results.

Pitfalls to Avoid When Using AEBT-T

During our development and initial presentations of this work, we have run into common points of confusion. In the discussion that follows, we list each of these points and clarify how they are handled within the manual.

1. *Acceptance does not mean teaching the client to accept one's hair pulling.*

Rather than viewing acceptance as the equivalent of a general unconditional acceptance for everything a person does, our definition of acceptance is specific. *Acceptance* refers to the acceptance of those uncontrollable internal experiences that lead to pulling, not acceptance of the pulling itself.

2. *Does blending the two interventions create confusion?*

On the one hand, individuals can view HRT/SC as very control-focused interventions, and they are correct. On the other, ACT is clearly not a control-focused strategy. We acknowledge the surface contradiction here, but there are clear distinctions that can eliminate confusion and provide specific benefits of blending the two approaches. The target of each intervention is different: HRT/SC procedures focus on eliminating and making more effortful *overt* behavior, whereas ACT focuses on *covert* or private experiences and supports overt behavior changes if such behavior interferes with one's values, which pulling often does.

There are a number of benefits to using both procedures. First, when implementing HRT/SC, clients may describe difficulties with implementation. They may say things such as "I tried, but it was too hard, the tension got too great," or "I had some really good days, but then I got in a fight with my husband and I went into a pulling episode to relax." Such statements provide therapeutic material on which ACT can be based. Second, in the ACT component, the client is challenged to do "behavioral commitment exercises," in which she seeks out high-risk pulling situations and practices being willing to experience the private events that show up for her. In this case, the client can be encouraged to use HRT/SC procedures as a tool to help control pulling during these exercises, thereby allowing the unpleasant private experiences to be present.

3. *Stimulus control interventions should focus only on making the pulling more difficult.*

Clinicians should take care when implementing SC procedures not to design SC interventions that specifically alleviate or prevent the unpleasant urges, emotions, or cognitions that precede pulling. The SC interventions should only be presented as a way to make the act of pulling more difficult. Describing SC interventions as a way to alleviate or prevent private experiences runs counter to the ACT philosophy and will likely undermine treatment efforts. In addition, the clinician should be flexible in the implementation of SC interventions. At certain points in the treatment, it may be desirable to stop SC interventions if they are found to be reducing the urge to pull.

4. *What is the role of values?*

Values are defined as engaging in actions on the basis of broad areas of life that are important to the client. These behaviors are done without regard for their effects on private events. We have used the term *quality of life* or *areas of importance* interchangeably. Values are also different from goals in that a value can never be reached—they function to guide behavior without end. Often clients and therapists become confused when discussing how pulling interferes with the client's working on her values. At the beginning of values work, the client will often say things like "I value having eyelashes," or "I value looking good." These are all worthy things to work toward, but the good clinician will work with the client to consider what pulling is taking the client away from. For example, if the client values being a good mother or spouse, yet engages in pulling for 3 hours per day, is that time spent being a good mother or a good spouse? Maybe letting go of controlling the urge would allow her to behave in a way that is consistent with her value of being a good mother.

Use of the Client Workbook

As with any behavior therapy, successful completion of homework and full participation in treatment are vital. To aid in the assignment and completion of homework and to encourage full participation, the client workbook has been created. The workbook contains all necessary materials to help the client successfully complete treatment. Specific forms include all necessary self-monitoring forms, checklists about antecedent and consequent cues to pulling, psychoeducational materials that can be read at the client's leisure, and various forms used to facilitate therapeutic exercises in and outside the session.

Chapter 2 *Assessment*

Assessment of TTM involves both initial assessment and ongoing monitoring of therapeutic progress. In this chapter we focus on the initial assessment. Assessment of progress throughout treatment is discussed in the description of individual sessions. This chapter does not present a comprehensive psychological assessment strategy, but rather provides a description of various assessment domains that clinicians who treat persons with TTM should consider. When possible, references to specific instruments are provided.

Pretreatment Assessment

Following the diagnosis of TTM, a pretreatment assessment should be conducted. This pretreatment assessment should focus on five areas: history of the disorder and prior attempts at treatment, description of current symptoms and their severity, functional assessment of pulling, comorbid conditions, and global life functioning.

History of Pulling and Prior Attempts at Treatment

Determine when and under what circumstances pulling started for your client and inquire about the client's previous attempts at treatment. Such information is useful in that it helps you to understand how the client views TTM in the context of her history and provides you with an understanding of how the client may view the therapeutic process (e.g., with mistrust, hope, doubt, etc.).

When asking clients about the earliest pulling episodes, one of two patterns will likely emerge. Clients typically state that pulling developed at either a very young age (e.g., 2–3 years old) and simply remained, or in early adolescence (e.g., 11–13 years old), with the pulling chronically waxing and waning since that time. Sometimes the first pulling episode can be vividly recalled, and sometimes the onset is vague. Occasionally, clients will relate pulling onset to a particularly stressful life situation (e.g., abuse, death of a parent, etc.). Although such life stressors may indeed be a trigger for some individuals, research does not support the occurrence of stressful life events as the trigger for all cases of TTM. It can also be useful to discuss early reactions to pulling. How did the child's parents respond? How did her peers react? Such information may be useful in helping the therapist understand how the client came to relate to her symptoms.

Because the current manual focuses on successful management of the current environment rather than correcting a past event, the client's historical account of pulling onset does not substantially influence implementation of AEBT-T. Nevertheless, historical information can be useful in forming a common basis of communication about the client's symptoms. It is also useful material for later exercises.

You should also be aware of the client's treatment history. Individuals diagnosed with TTM will likely have a long history with the disorder. Onset typically occurs in early adolescence, and for many the disorder is chronic. Likewise, adults with TTM are likely to have attempted and failed multiple treatments, including medications, diets, and therapies. This chronicity is in part due to TTM being a difficult disorder to treat and in part to most mental health professionals not being sufficiently trained in its treatment (Marcks, Wetterneck, & Woods, 2006). Therefore, it is likely that clients will be hopeful, but skeptical, of therapists' abilities to serve as an agent of change. You should be open and appreciative of the client's likely frustration with prior attempts at treatment.

Description of Current Symptoms and Severity

It is important to develop an understanding of the client's pulling and to assess its severity. Table 2.1 lists areas where pulling can occur and in-

Table 2.1 Pulling Site Checklist and Percentage of Those with TTM Who Endorse Site as a Pulling Site

Site	Yes	No	Normative %
Scalp	☐	☐	73
Eyebrows	☐	☐	56
Eyelashes	☐	☐	52
Pubic region	☐	☐	51
Legs	☐	☐	22
Arms	☐	☐	12
Armpits	☐	☐	12
Trunk	☐	☐	7
Moustache	☐	☐	5
Beard	☐	☐	4
Cheek, chin	☐	☐	2
Fingers	☐	☐	1
Pets, animals	☐	☐	.5
Breasts, nipples	☐	☐	.5
Back	☐	☐	.2
Feet, toes	☐	☐	.9
Other people	☐	☐	.4
Beauty or birth marks	☐	☐	.1
Nose	☐	☐	.8
Ear	☐	☐	.4
Neck	☐	☐	.5
Stomach	☐	☐	.2
Shoulder	☐	☐	.1
Chest	☐	☐	.2
Bottom, perineum	☐	☐	.3

cludes the prevalence of pulling, from each area, found in the general TTM population.

As can be seen, pulling is most likely to occur on the scalp, eyelashes, and eyebrows. Although quite common, pubic pulling is not readily disclosed, and the astute clinician should ask about its occurrence, while recognizing the sensitive nature of the question. Damage from pulling may vary from complete baldness, to fairly well-distributed thinning of hair, to no noticeable damage. Some people pull often from one area and others may pull a little from many areas. The clinician should also note that hair is not always pulled from the client's own body. Pulling the hair of significant others, children, pets, or toys such as stuffed animals or dolls can also occur.

In addition to assessing areas of the body from which hair is removed, attempt to understand how the pulling sequence starts and what the client does with the hair after it is pulled.

Individuals with TTM may enact a host of hair-related behaviors prior to the actual removal of hair. Table 2.2 describes the most common ones. For each client, attempt to develop an understanding of these behaviors along with the behavioral sequence that leads to the removal of the hair. After identifying the pre-pulling sequence, determine what the client does with the hair after it is pulled.

Post-pulling behaviors vary widely. Table 2.2 lists activities that the client may do after pulling the hair. Although the list is not comprehensive, it does represent more commonly seen activities. As the table clearly demonstrates, a wide variety of post-pulling behaviors can occur, but one is particularly important to note. If a client informs you that she is ingesting the hair, refer the client to a physician to assess for the possible development of a trichobezoar, which is a mass of hair and food particles that can form in persons who ingest pulled hair.

After assessing the pre- and post-pulling behaviors, it is helpful to obtain baseline measures of pulling severity. The following are descriptions of commonly accepted TTM severity measures.

The *Massachusetts General Hospital Hairpulling Scale* (MGH-HS; Keuthen et al., 1995) is a seven-question self-report measure that assesses global hair-pulling severity. Each item is rated on a scale of 0–4, and the total

---

Table 2.2 Examples of Pre- and Post-Pulling Behaviors

Pre-Pulling Behaviors

Stroking the hair
Twisting or playing with the hair
Mouthing hair
Staring or gazing at the hair
Isolating one or two hairs
Finding a thick hair
Finding a rough or coarse hair
Finding a discolored hair
Finding a nonsymmetrical (out of place) hair

Post-Pulling Behaviors

Rubbing pulled hair on mouth
Placing pulled hair in the mouth
Biting pulled hair
Listening for the "pop" sound when hair is removed
Ingesting pulled hair
Rubbing pulled hair between fingers
Wrapping pulled hair around fingers
Discarding hairs
"Popping" root of hair
Doing something with the pulled root
Examining the pulled hair
Saving the pulled hair or part of pulled hair

---

severity score is created by summing the seven items. Total severity scores range from 0 to 28, with higher scores reflecting greater severity. The instrument has been found to have acceptable psychometric properties (Keuthen et al., 1995; O'Sullivan et al., 1995). In addition to the total severity score, recent research (Keuthen et al., 2007) suggests that the MGH-HS contains two factorially derived subscales, including one measuring severity (obtained by summing items 1, 2, 4, and 7), and one measuring resistance and control (obtained by summing items, 3, 5, and 6). One caveat that should be recognized is that the MGH-HS is based on a different framework than the ACT model. The MGH-HS was developed within a traditional cognitive-behavior therapy framework and includes questions about the degree to which the urges have reduced and how much control the client has over the urge, both of which are seen as signs of therapeutic improvement. In the ACT model, the client is discouraged from controlling the urge. As a result, the MGH-HS can be confusing to the client as she progresses through AEBT-T, and it may underestimate improvement. Because a more appropriate measure of overall severity does not exist, the MGH-HS is still used in AEBT-T outcome studies, but clinicians should be aware of its limitations, potential for confusion with clients, and likelihood of underestimating improvement.

The *National Institute of Mental Health* (NIMH) *Trichotillomania Scales* (Swedo et al., 1989) comprise this semi-structured clinical interview. There is a clinician-rated scale, the NIMH-TTM Symptom Severity Scale (NIMH-TSS), and an overall impairment scale, the NIMH-Trichotillomania Impairment Scale (NIMH-TIS). The NIMH-TSS consists of five items of assessment: time spent pulling, problems thinking about pulling, attempts to resist the urge to pull, general distress about the pulling, and the interference in one's life created by pulling. The NIMH-TIS is a 10-point, clinician-completed rating scale measuring impairment produced by the time spent pulling or concealing damage, ability to control pulling, severity of alopecia, interference, and incapacitation caused by the pulling. Although few data exist for the psychometric properties of the NIMH-TTM Scales, the interrater reliability scores for the measure have been found to range from .78 to .81 when the scales were administered to the same clients by different raters. In addition, these scales appear to be sensitive to change in symptom severity as a result of treatment (Swedo et al., 1989). Limitations of the NIMH-TSS are similar to those of the MGH-HS; there are inconsistencies between some items of the NIMH-TSS and the principles of ACT. Therapists should be aware of these contradictions.

In *product measurement*, another method of assessing pulling severity, the product of pulling is measured. *Products* are physical traces that remain as a result of a behavior. In TTM, common product measures include the diameter of bald spots, rating of the damage from areas of pulling, the number of pulled hairs, or pulled hairs collected by the client and returned to the therapist. Although product measures can be quite useful and informative, clinicians should approach them with caution. It is often quite shameful and embarrassing for clients to let their damaged area be seen by others, let alone measured, and it is often equally difficult for them to collect the pulled hair and bring it to therapy. The upside of these procedures is that they are less likely to be fictitious, and when regrowth starts to occur, product measurement can be particularly reinforcing.

In *self-monitoring*, the most common strategy for assessing pulling severity, the client monitors her own pulling. Monitoring can be done contingent on each pulling episode, or globally at the end of each day. In addition to providing a measure of pulling frequency, self-monitoring can also be helpful in collecting other data about particular environmental variables that may influence the behavior.

Functional Assessment of Pulling

It is important to understand the function that pulling plays for an individual client. Therefore you should conduct a functional assessment, to determine settings in which pulling commonly occurs, emotional states or cognitions with which pulling is associated, and both internal and social consequences that may occur as a result of pulling, all of which may serve to maintain the behavior. In the following discussion we briefly review the various content domains that should be considered in a functional assessment of TTM.

Settings

Various settings and activities have been associated with increased frequency of pulling. These include studying, reading, doing homework, watching television, being alone, having leisure time, and grooming (Mackenzie, Ristvedt, Christenson, Smith Lebow, & Mitchell, 1995). Other research shows that pulling tends to be worse in the evening (du Toit et al., 2001) and when traveling or waiting for something to happen (O'Conner, Brisebois, Brault, Robillard, & Loiselle, 2003). Likewise, it is not uncommon to hear clients report that pulling most frequently occurs in the bathroom, bedroom, den, or car. Settings in which the client can be alone and in which she is at a period of low activity often lead to more pulling.

Antecedent Emotional States

Researchers have long recognized the association between various antecedent states and pulling severity. Emotional states linked to increased levels of pulling include boredom, tension, and anxiety (Diefenbach et al., 2002). In addition to these more discreet emotional states, it is common to hear clients report a vague urge to pull, an itchy feeling (du Toit et al., 2001), or generally negative affect (e.g., shame) prior to pulling episodes.

Antecedent Cognitions

At times, clients may hold specific beliefs and thought patterns that may serve to evoke or maintain pulling if taken literally and acted upon. Examples include beliefs about the inappropriateness of certain hairs (e.g., too thick, too coarse, too gray), thoughts that hairlines should be symmetrical, beliefs that hair pulling is uncontrollable, thoughts that if pulling has started it will be impossible to stop, mind-reading thoughts in which the client assumes others view her appearance negatively, and thoughts that she is unworthy or unlovable because of her appearance.

Consequences of Pulling

Various changes in the client's environment can take place during a pulling episode. Generally, these are divided into internal and external consequences. Internal consequences are those autonomic, tactile, auditory, or cognitive changes within the client herself that stem from pulling. Examples include reduction of an urge, relief, tension reduction, decreases in anxiety, confidence that the "bad" hair has been removed, tactile sensations stemming from rubbing the hair on the lips or between the fingers, the sound of the hair being pulled or bitten, etc. External consequences are social reactions to the pulling that may occur. Parents or significant others may comment on the pulling, the client may be told repeatedly to stop the behavior, or the pulling activity may disrupt ongoing activities that need to be completed.

Conducting a careful functional assessment focusing on internal and external antecedents and consequences will provide useful examples throughout treatment, will be helpful in fleshing out the client's description of her pulling, and will be particularly useful in developing the later SC interventions described in the manual.

Self-Report Measures

In addition to obtaining an individualized functional assessment, two self-report measures may aid in determining the relative levels of focused (emotion-controlling) and automatic pulling. These instruments are described below. Although they are not intended to supplant a good functional assessment, they are potentially useful complementary instruments.

The *Milwaukee Inventory of Subtypes of Trichotillomania Scale-Adult* (MIST-A; Flessner et al., in press) is a 15-item scale consisting of two separate subscales. The Focused Pulling Scale consists of 10 items designed to measure focused pulling symptoms of TTM. It has an internal consistency of ($\propto = .77$), and higher scores on the Focused scale are correlated with greater levels of depression, anxiety, and stress on the DASS-21 (Lovibond & Lovibond, 1995), along with a greater likelihood to pull in response to physical anxiety, specific bodily sensations, and worry. The Automatic Pulling Scale is a five-item scale designed to measure the level of automatic pulling symptoms of TTM. It has an internal consistency of ($\propto = .73$) and is inversely correlated with the percentage of pulling episodes in which participants were aware of their pulling. The Automatic Pulling Scale was not correlated with the DASS-21 subscales, nor was it correlated with one's self-reported likelihood to pull in response to physical anxiety, a specific bodily sensation, and worry. Each item on the MIST-A is rated from 0 ("not true of any of my hair pulling") to 9 ("true for all of my hair pulling"). Based on a normative sample of 1,697 individuals reporting behaviors consistent with a diagnosis of TTM, mean Focused Pulling Scale scores were 45.4, $SD = 16.2$. Mean Automatic Pulling Scale scores were 25.7, $SD = 9.04$. The Focused and Automatic subscales are not significantly correlated, which suggests that they measure separate processes. We have included a copy of the MIST-A in Appendix A. You may photocopy the scale from the book or download copies from the Treatments *ThatWork*™ Web site at www.oup.com/us/ttw.

The *Acceptance and Action Questionnaire* (AAQ; Hayes et al., 2004) is a nine-item measure of acceptance of private events or experiential avoidance. The AAQ has been shown to be internally consistent. A significant pre–post decrease in AAQ scores suggests that the subject has become more open to experiencing unpleasant private events and has become less likely to use emotional control strategies. The AAQ has adequate internal consistency (coefficient alpha = .70; Hayes et al., 2004). The AAQ has a reported mean in nonclinical samples of 33.29 and *SD* of 6.93. The AAQ was developed as a general clinical measure, but it usually is more sensitive to change when adjusted for a particular disorder. While the psychometrics of the original AAQ no longer apply, a clinician may find that the version adjusted for TTM (AAQ-4TTM) is more clinically useful. We provide both the standard AAQ and a TTM-specific version of the AAQ in Appendix A. You may photocopy the questionnaires from the book or download copies from the Treatments *ThatWork*™ Web site at www.oup.com/us/ttw.

Comorbid Conditions and Differential Diagnoses

As psychiatric comorbidity rates are high in TTM populations, it is important to conduct a good assessment for co-occurring conditions. Three areas should be considered. The first involves differential diagnosis. Assuming physical causes for hair loss have been ruled out (e.g., alopecia, male pattern baldness, etc.), the astute clinician will consider the possibility of various differential diagnoses. Three specific diagnoses should be considered: OCD, body dysmorphic disorder (BDD), and a psychotic disorder. Individuals who pull in response to specific intrusive and unwanted obsessions may be considered for an OCD diagnosis if their pulling functions to reduce the anxiety. Nevertheless, hair pulling as a primary compulsion is rare, and in the absence of a history of other compulsive behaviors or in the absence of obsessional content, it is unlikely that the pulling is a result of OCD.

Body dysmorphic disorder is another common differential diagnosis. Those with BDD are preoccupied with an imagined defect in appearance (American Psychiatric Association, 2000). In those individuals who pull, a BDD diagnosis would be considered only if the pulling occurred in reaction to, or as a way to correct, a perceived deficit in appearance. The presence of automatic pulling or pulling for pulling's sake would clearly argue against a BDD diagnosis. Finally, clinicians should probe for the possibility that pulling could be the result of hallucinations (e.g., visual or tactile hallucinations of bugs crawling on or into the skin) or delusions (e.g., beliefs that hairs are conduits for information to be implanted into the brain). Although such symptom presentations are rare, the clinician should be aware of the possibility, as such diagnoses require different treatments.

Co-occurring conditions should also be assessed for how they contribute to the worsening of TTM symptoms. For example, a high level of trait anxiety may set the occasion for a considerable amount of focused pulling. Finally, clinicians should be aware of how TTM contributes to other conditions. In one recent survey, 70% of those with the disorder felt that TTM had contributed to the development of another psychiatric disorder.

Global Life Functioning

The primary area affected by TTM is quality of life. Unlike other disorders such as depression or schizophrenia, in which the target behavior is itself labeled as aversive (e.g., most people do not like the feeling of being depressed), many people with TTM enjoy the pulling. We have heard many clients say, "I would love to pull for hours each night if it didn't cause these bald patches." The part of TTM that brings most clients into therapy is the amount of time that pulling takes away from their day, the restriction of activities from having bald spots, and, for many, the guilt and embarrassment that come with pulling. In short, the primary negative result of hair pulling is the difficulty it brings to doing many things that are important in life. It is clinically useful for both the client and the therapist to be aware of the areas of life that are being restricted by the pulling or by avoiding things that occasion the urge to pull. While this is formally assessed in the AEBT-T protocol, there are standardized measures for quality of life that may be useful.

Summary

The assessment approach outlined in this chapter reflects procedures that can be useful to paint an initial picture of the client's struggle. Nevertheless, it should be understood that assessment does not end here. Ongoing assessment of pulling reduction is necessary, but perhaps even more important is continual assessment of how the client is functioning globally. Is she doing things she didn't do before because of the pulling? Is she living a more fulfilling life? If not, this is why people come to treatment, and clinicians should keep this in mind throughout all aspects of therapy.

Chapter 3 · Session 1: Trichotillomania (TTM) Education, Therapy Overview, Expectations, and Stimulus Control Assessment

(Corresponds to chapter 1 of the workbook)

Materials Needed

■ Trichotillomania Education Handout

■ Stimulus Control Assessment Form (SCAF)

■ TTM Self-Monitoring Form

■ Monitoring Your Urge Form

Session Outline

■ Conduct weekly assessment of progress

■ Provide education about TTM

■ Provide overview of the program

■ Discuss therapeutic expectations

■ Introduce patient to habit reversal training (HRT) and stimulus control

■ Conduct stimulus control assessment

■ Introduce self-monitoring and assign homework

Completion of Assessment Measures

At the start of every session, the client should turn in or complete a weekly assessment. No specific weekly assessment is noted in this manual to allow flexibility, but we prefer a product measure or self-report of hairs pulled plus the MIST-A. The various TTM assessments described in Chapter 2 can be tailored to suit the client's needs. The corresponding workbook includes copies of the MIST-A, as well as of the AAQ and the AAQ-4TTM. It can be useful to plot data from these measures on a graph on a weekly basis and review the graph with the client. Not only can it serve as a reinforcing event for client progress, but lack of improvement can be used to initiate discussion about where the client is experiencing difficulties. A blank graph for tracking assessment data on a week-by-week basis can be found at the back of the workbook. Also included in the workbook is a daily graph for each week of therapy. This graph can be used to plot daily progress as shown on the client's completed TTM Self-Monitoring forms and can be useful in facilitating discussion about various events related to more or less pulling.

TTM Education

At the start of Session 1, refer the client to the TTM educational material in Chapter 1 of the workbook. The purpose of the educational component is to make sure the client has a basic understanding of TTM and to let her know that she is not alone in experiencing the disorder. Review and discuss all aspects of TTM including its definition, common areas from which hair is pulled, prevalence and gender differences in TTM, common comorbid conditions, the typical age of onset, patterns of pulling, and genetic and biological factors in the development of pulling. Also review with the client the distinction between focused and automatic pulling (see Chapter 1). This discussion will set the stage for the general description of the treatment program.

A copy of the TTM Education Handout is provided in Appendix B.

Overview of Treatment

Describe the basic premise of treatment, but avoid getting into protracted discussions or debates with the client over the utility of various components for her specific pattern of pulling. The description of treatment should be brief and serve to give the client a general notion of the process. You may use the following sample dialogue to introduce the treatment:

> As we just discussed, pulling can be either focused or automatic, and in many cases, people with TTM have both styles. Although the difference between these two is important because it leads us to develop more effective treatments, the truth is that it is often difficult to tell when a pulling episode is focused or automatic. For that reason, we won't spend too much time worrying about whether a particular episode is focused or automatic. We'll simply do the treatments that were developed for each type. Next week, we will start doing the treatments that were designed specifically to stop your pulling. In weeks 3 through 8, we will be asking you to look at your thoughts, feelings, emotions, and urges to pull a little differently. During this time, we will continue to work on ways to stop pulling and will also increase our attention on some of the personal variables that play into your pulling. During weeks 9 and 10, we'll review what we have learned and discuss ways for you to keep your progress going.
>
> During each of our sessions, I'll ask be asking you to do work in session and homework outside of the session. Even if you feel that a specific exercise is silly or doesn't pertain to you, I'll ask you to withhold judgment and participate in the exercises. Do you have any questions? Okay. Let's talk a little more about what we can expect as we go through this process together.

Therapeutic Expectations

Discuss with the client her expectations for treatment. In discussion of expectations, three issues should be addressed. First, the therapist and client should begin to set up the distinction between urges and actual pulling. Second, the client should understand that the treatment is active and involves learning new skills and that she should not judge the outcome impulsively. Third, the client should understand that during treatment, she will be asked to participate in various exercises and work hard but that she will not be forced to do anything she doesn't agree to do.

The client likely sees therapy as being just about reducing pulling. Inform her that the first part of therapy focuses on getting the *act of pulling* under control, and Sessions 3 through 10 will focus on what to do with her *urges to pull*. Making this distinction will be difficult because the urges to pull and the act of pulling are usually tightly linked, if not synonymous, in the client's mind. To help separate the urges from the act of pulling, relevant homework is assigned in Sessions 1–3. In these assignments, the client is asked to describe her urges to pull and what she does when they are present. This information will be used later in therapy. The following is a sample dialogue establishing expectations.

> *This treatment is very active. You will be asked but not forced to do many exercises, some of which may be difficult. These exercises will focus on stopping your pulling and addressing your urges to pull. We treat the pulling and the urges to pull as separate things. I know they are probably not separate in your mind, but we are going to address them one at a time. Because this is different from how you probably see your TTM, this therapy can be demanding, and it can be confusing. I can't fully describe this approach to you because to some degree the explaining happens during therapy.*

> *This first part of therapy deals with getting your pulling under control. As you work on stopping your pulling, you will find that your urges to pull will go up and down. In Session 4 we will work on your struggle with your urges to pull and the ways that you respond to them. Many therapists who treat TTM would work with you to change or regulate your pulling and your urges to pull at the same time. They may try to find other ways you haven't considered to help reduce your urges to pull. These are certainly potentially viable options. Many people with TTM try this approach, either on their own or with the help of a therapist. Some find it useful and some do not. If you've tried it, I'm guessing that it has not worked out for you because you are still looking for help. This treatment is not about giving you one more way to try and reduce the urges to pull—it's different. Starting this week, I'm going to ask you to start tracking your urges or thoughts about pulling and what you do with them when they show up. I am going to ask you to just do what you normally do when your urges to pull show up, and I really want you to pay close attention. We will use this information in Session 4.*

You might get frustrated or feel anxious during this initial part of therapy. My experience with this approach is that it can put you on a bit of a roller coaster. All kinds of different emotions might emerge: interest, boredom, anxiety, sadness, clarity, confusion, and so on. I don't want to push you into something that you are not willing to do. Working on something that is as big in your life as hair pulling should not be entered into lightly.

It is often wise to get the client to commit to a course of treatment and agree not to measure progress impulsively. The full benefits will likely be seen after both automatic and focused pulling are targeted. Notice that there is no indication that her urges to pull will decrease. Such a goal is not a focus of this treatment. Avoid making that promise because it will conflict with the second phase of this therapy. You may use the following sample dialogue with the client:

In this treatment, you and I will work as a team. Remember, whenever you learn to do something new, it is tough and frustrating at first, but there is a nice payoff at the end. Remember when you first learned to ride a bicycle. You fell over and over again. You scraped your knees, bumped your head, and bruised your arms. You had to think about every move you made as you tried to balance and keep pedaling. But eventually, you learned to ride. You were able to go riding with your friends and maybe you are still into cycling. Therapy is like that. It is tough and demanding, but we are doing it because it is important to you; your hair pulling has likely been holding you back from other things quite a lot. During treatment, you'll fall, you'll feel a bit confused, and you'll probably get frustrated at times, but I hope it will provide you with something important at the end. Like most good things in life, success in treatment is not easy to achieve; it will take work. I tell you this because I'd like you to commit to working hard for the 10 sessions we have planned. Let's push ahead for that amount of time no matter what—even if you really want to quit. Then we will stop and look at your situation. If at that time it looks as though we aren't making progress, we will do something else.

The client is also given a little warning that the second part of therapy is more interactive and less didactic. This helps prepare the client for the

ACT phase of therapy. It also conveys that the therapist is open to what the client thinks and feels about the therapy.

> From the beginning until about the middle of therapy, I'm going to be doing a lot of the talking. Although this isn't the way therapy usually happens, it's necessary here, because what we'll be discussing can be very different from what you're used to hearing. It's like when you're building a house—first you have to lay a solid foundation. We need to build our foundation. We need to speak the same language, and the early part of treatment will give us this common language. However, I don't want you to get too comfortable with me doing most of the talking because this will change, and by the end, you will be doing most of the talking. A final thing we need to be clear on is that even though I will be doing much of the talking early on, you need to stay active. Remember, we are working together as a team, and if you don't understand something, you need to tell me. If you think I'm wrong, I need to know that too. Let me know what you're thinking and what you're feeling.

Introduction to Habit Reversal Therapy and Stimulus Control Procedures

Introduce HRT to the client as a technique that is useful in stopping the act of pulling. You may use the following sample dialogue:

> Now, we're going to start a piece of the treatment that was developed to help you stop pulling. The treatment that gives you strategies for stopping the act of pulling involves learning two skills. The first is called habit reversal. Habit reversal will bring the pulling more into your awareness and give you a way to stop it.

Also provide the client with a rationale for stimulus control procedures.

> The second skill is called stimulus control. The purpose of stimulus control is to find things that make pulling more difficult for you to do. We know that when behavior becomes more difficult it happens less. So our goal in stimulus control is to come up with relatively simple strategies in your life that you can use to make your pulling more effortful. At this point, I'd like to discuss with you the various situations that make your pulling more or less likely to happen.

Stimulus Control Assessment

Using the Stimulus Control Assessment Form (SCAF) in Appendix B, engage the client in an assessment of the different situations that make pulling more likely. Pay specific attention to those settings or items that can be altered in the future.

End the session by introducing self-monitoring, assigning homework, and telling the client that the next session will involve the implementation of HRT and SC procedures.

Introducing Self-Monitoring and Assigning Homework

Throughout the course of treatment, the client will be asked to monitor her pulling. This is intended to serve two purposes. First, it will provide ongoing data to the therapist on results of the treatment. Second it will keep the client invested in the therapeutic endeavor. To introduce the monitoring and assign the homework for the first week, the following could be said:

> From now until the end of treatment, I'm going to ask you to monitor your pulling for me. During the next week, I'd like you to use the TTM Self-Monitoring Form in the workbook to record any pulling you do during the day. Before you go to bed each night, I would like you to record how much time you spent pulling each day, describe the situations in which your pulling occurred, and describe the common thoughts, emotions, and urges you had before and after you pulled. I'd like you to bring the completed form back to me at our next session. Do you have any questions?

> I'd also like you to complete the Monitoring Your Urge Form. To do this, I'd like you to note three times each day when you had an urge to pull your hair. For each of these times, please write down what you did to deal with the urge, if you did anything. At the next session, I'd like you to bring the completed form back to me. Keep in mind that we are just paying attention to this part of your trichotillomania; we are not going to do anything with it at this time. Do you have any questions?

Homework

✎ Instruct client to monitor hair pulling on a daily basis using the TTM Self-Monitoring Form in the workbook.

✎ Instruct the client to complete the Monitoring Your Urge Form in the workbook on a daily basis over the course of the next week.

Chapter 4

Session 2: Habit Reversal Training and Stimulus Control Procedures

(Corresponds to chapter 2 of the workbook)

Materials Needed

- Stimulus Control Assignment Sheet

Session Outline

- Conduct weekly assessment of progress
- Inquire about any reactions to material from previous session
- Review homework
- Implement HRT
- Recommend specific stimulus control interventions
- Assign homework

Completion of Assessment Measures

As in every session, the client should return or complete an assessment to gauge progress. This progress (or lack of it) and the client's reactions should be discussed. Help the client plot assessment data on the weekly graph provided in the workbook.

Review of Previous Material

Answer any questions the client may have about TTM or the treatment program.

Homework Review

Review the client's completed TTM Self-Monitoring Form and Monitoring Your Urge Form from the preceding week. Give praise for doing the homework and point out the importance of continued monitoring. Plot the self-monitoring data on the daily graph (in the workbook) to examine fluctuations in pulling. Discuss patterns and trends in the data. For example, the client may report more pulling in the evening before going to bed, or more pulling following stressful days at work. She may report having thoughts that a particular type of hair needs to be removed. Such information can be useful in understanding how the pulling works for that particular patient. Give the client an opportunity to acknowledge any reactions she may have had to her pulling.

Habit Reversal Training

Inform the client that HRT will be implemented in today's session. Reiterate that HRT is being done to help develop control over the act of pulling and that the accompanying urges should be monitored. HRT is implemented in two parts: awareness training and competing response training.

Awareness Training

The purpose of awareness training is to help the client recognize and react to episodes of the pulling or antecedent stimuli. Provide the client with a rationale for awareness training prior to its implementation. An example of a rationale follows:

> *The first part of HRT is to teach you to know when you pull. We are going to make you aware of when it is happening. Because the rest of the treatment depends on you knowing exactly when pulling is about to happen or has happened, this is a very important part of the treatment. Today we're doing exercises that will make you very aware of your pulling.*

Awareness training involves describing the pulling, describing the sensations and behaviors that precede the pulling, acknowledging therapist-simulated pulling, and acknowledging real or simulated pulling exhibited by the client. Each of these specific procedures is outlined here.

Describing the Pulling

This is accomplished by having the client give a detailed description of what the pulling looks like. Sometimes this can be enhanced by having the client simulate a pulling episode in the mirror. If the client fails to describe a key feature of the pulling, be sure to point this out.

The description of pulling should be elaborated on until you feel that the pulling and any associated behaviors have been described in sufficient detail. When a complete description has been provided, have the client describe sensations and behaviors that precede the pulling.

Describing Preceding Sensations and Behaviors

The purpose of this procedure is to have the client cue in on precursory sensations and behaviors that may inform her that the pulling is about to occur. These precursory sensations and behaviors are "warning signs," or "pulling signals." The topic could be introduced as follows:

> *To be really aware of a problem, you need to know when it's happening and when it's about to happen. In the case of pulling, your body is probably sending you signals, or "warning signs," before you pull to let you know that pulling is about to start. What I want you to do next is to really think about these signals. These can be things you do or things you feel.*

There may be several warning signs such as bringing one's hand toward the head, sitting in a specific position, stroking the hair, or searching for the "right" hair to pull. In addition, there will likely be private warning signs such as an urge to pull or a thought about the appropriateness of a particular hair for pulling. Work with the client to establish one to three different warning signs she may experience. If the client denies experiencing warning signs, point out a few of the examples listed previously and ask the client if she experiences any of these signs. If the client still denies the presence of warning signs, move to the next awareness training procedure, acknowledging therapist-simulated pulling.

Acknowledging Therapist-Simulated Pulling

The purpose of this procedure is to help the client begin to acknowledge pulling. In this procedure, the client will be asked to verbally acknowledge occurrences of her own pulling as simulated by the therapist. A rationale could be given as follows:

> *Now we're going to practice being aware of the pulling. We'll start by having you point out my pulling, because sometimes it's easier for people to get the hang of this when they're watching someone else. During the next few minutes of our discussion, I'll be acting out some of your pulling. As soon as you see me pull, just raise your finger to let me know you caught it.*

Continue this exercise until you feel the client can successfully acknowledge your simulated attempts at pulling. When the client correctly identifies the simulated pulling, provide praise for correct acknowledgment. If there are instances when you simulate pulling and the client does not acknowledge it, be sure to let her know that pulling had just occurred. It may be helpful to explain the exercise and review the instructions once more.

Next, repeat this process with the previously identified warning signs. The process is simple with overt warning signs (e.g., hands moving up toward the scalp), but obviously difficult to do with the private warning signs (e.g., an urge or thought). In such cases, warning sign detection is done for the overt signs only. Each warning sign need not be addressed separately; rather, they can be interspersed with each other. You may use the following sample dialogue to introduce this to the client:

> *You did a great job pointing out my pulling. Now we're going to do the same thing with the signals you told me about. You also need to be able to point out warning signs, because they will let you know that the pulling is coming. Again, during the next few minutes of our dis-*

cussion, I'll be acting out your different signals. Do you remember
what they were? As soon as you see me do any one of them, I want
you to raise your finger.

Again, continue this exercise until you feel the client is reliably able to detect your simulated warning signs. After the client has successfully acknowledged the presence of simulated pulling and warning signs, the client is ready to do the final step in awareness training, acknowledging self-pulling.

Acknowledging Self-Pulling

This procedure is nearly identical to the previous procedure, except the client will be asked to point out occurrences of her own pulling and warning signs. The most difficult part of this procedure is getting the client to pull. Often the client does not pull during sessions. In such cases, ask the client to simulate her own pulling and warning signs. The procedure can be introduced as follows:

You did an excellent job pointing out my pulling. Now I want you to
start pointing out your own. We're going to talk about different things
for the next 10 minutes or so. Right after you pull, I want you to raise
a finger.

In cases where the client is not pulling in session, the following sample dialogue can be used.

Therapist: You did an excellent job pointing out my "pulling." Now I want you to start pointing out your own. Do you think you'll actually pull in front of me today?

Client: No, I really don't pull in front of anyone.

Therapist: That's okay. It's common for people with TTM to not pull in public. Regardless, it can sometimes be helpful if you get used to pulling or at least starting to pull, and then stopping to notice that it's happening. To help you practice this, I'd like you to pretend to pull once in a while, as we're talking for the next 10 minutes or so. Right after you pretend to pull, I want you to raise a finger. This may feel a bit awkward, but just give it your best shot.

Again, provide praise for correct acknowledgment, and feedback and repeated instructions when the client fails to acknowledge pulling that has occurred. Continue the exercise until you feel the client is accurately acknowledging her own pulling. Repeat the procedure, having the client acknowledge warning signs rather than pulling. Use similar dialogue to that described previously if it's unlikely the person will enact warning signs during the session.

Upon completion of the four awareness-training procedures, the client is ready to begin the primary component of HRT, competing response training (CRT).

Competing Response Training

Competing response training is at the center of HRT. A competing response is a behavior that has three characteristics. First, it is physically incompatible with the pulling. When the client is faithfully doing the competing response, she cannot be pulling. Second, it is something that the client can do easily in almost any situation. Third, it is something the client can do that is not noticeable to others. One of the most common competing responses for hair pulling, and the one we used in our studies of this treatment program, involved asking the client to put her arms down at her sides and gently clench her fists for 1 minute whenever her hands started to go toward the scalp or when she experienced the urge to pull. Other examples of competing responses for pulling include folding the arms together, putting one's hands in pockets, or folding one's hands.

When introducing this concept, be sure that the chosen competing response is acceptable to the client. Forcing the client to agree to unacceptable competing responses often translates into poor treatment compliance. One way of introducing the competing-response phase and asking about its acceptability is as follows:

We're now at the main part of HRT. We're going to learn something called the competing response. In here we'll call these your "exercises." The purpose of these exercises is to give you something to prevent your pulling from happening. After you do this long enough it becomes very natural and the pulling decreases. I'll show you the exercise in a few minutes. Basically, you will be expected to do this exercise for 1 minute each time you pull or notice one of your signals we talked about earlier.

Demonstrate the chosen competing response.

Well, you've seen the exercise you'll be expected to do. Remember, you'll be asked to do this for 1 minute each time you pull or notice a signal. Before we continue, I want to make sure that you're willing to do this exercise. I know that the exercise may not feel natural yet, but you will get better at it. Right now, I'm wondering if you think it will work for you when you have to do it for real. Do you foresee any situations in which the exercise will be impossible or you won't be willing to do it?

Discuss with the client any concerns she may have about using a competing response. Work with the client to develop strategies for addressing these concerns. If the problems with the chosen competing response are insurmountable, choose another.

Teaching the Competing Response

Teach the client to implement the competing response for 1 minute, contingent on occurrences of pulling or warning signs. Demonstrate how the competing response should be implemented contingent on pulling and pulling signals.

Well, you've seen me do this, now it's your turn. We've already reviewed the exercises and you seem to be doing that very well. Now, we need to use the exercises to stop your pulling. Remember the two times you are to use your exercises for 1 minute are 1) as soon as you pull and 2) as soon as you notice one of your pulling signals. As soon as either one of these two things happen, you should stop and begin your exercises.

What I'd like you to do is to pretend to pull and then do the exercise for 1 minute. After that I'll ask you to go through each of your pulling signals and show me how you would do the exercise.

Ask the client to demonstrate the competing response after simulated pulling and pulling signals. If she does this correctly, be sure to offer praise and encouragement. However, if you recognize that the client is doing something incorrectly, provide corrective feedback.

Using HRT

Describe to the client how the HRT procedures should be implemented. This involves doing the competing response contingent on any of the pulling signals and/or when the pulling has already started. The competing response should be done for 1 minute. If the pulling or warning sign recurs immediately after the minute is up, the competing response should be done for another minute.

To the new client it may often feel that she is doing the competing response continuously, which can lead to frustration. Warn the client about this possibility. Finally, when the client starts seeing improvement, she may become less vigilant about implementing the exercises. It is useful to caution against these two possibilities.

Stimulus Control Procedures

After identifying the various factors that make pulling more likely to occur, you should select various interventions that make pulling more difficult. A list of various interventions can be found at the end of the chapter, but feel free to create new ones as appropriate for your client. However, keep in mind that any stimulus control interventions you choose should adhere to the following three principles. First, stimulus control techniques should not be done or framed as a way to prevent or avoid the emergence of uncomfortable urges, feelings, or thoughts. Such strategies are counterproductive to the AEBT-T model. Second, the stimulus control interventions should be simple, easy to implement, and, when possible, not socially disruptive. Third, the stimulus control interventions are done to make pulling more difficult or burdensome.

After selecting the individualized stimulus control techniques, work with the client to complete the Stimulus Control Assignment Sheet in

Chapter 2 of the workbook. As an example of a stimulus control intervention, assume a client is more likely to pull her eyebrows when in a brightly lit bathroom, removing makeup from her face, and standing very close to the mirror, but to pull her scalp hair while reading books. In this case, to make eyebrow pulling more difficult, instruct the client to remove her makeup in a different room, with less lighting, while standing further away from the mirror. Clients who use hand-held mirrors, compacts, or tweezers to facilitate pulling may be asked to discard or give away these items. To make the scalp pulling more effortful, the participant may be encouraged to use books on tape, read while wearing mittens, or hold the book with both hands. You may have to be creative in devising ways to alter various stimuli. Be careful not to make these procedures too difficult, or compliance may be lower. Remember, none of these things should be done with the intention of eliminating, reducing, or preventing the urge to pull (though this may happen). Rather, the stimulus control techniques should only be done to make pulling more difficult.

Homework

✎ Instruct the client to continue monitoring hair-pulling episodes and what the client does with her urges to pull over the course of the next week using the TTM Self-Monitoring Form and Monitoring Your Urge Form in the workbook.

✎ Ask the client to engage in a competing response whenever she pulls, is about to pull, or experiences one of the pulling signals.

✎ Have the client begin using stimulus control procedures.

Stimulus Control Intervention Recommendations

The Stimulus Control Assessment Form (SCAF) is designed to be completed during Session 1 of AEBT-T. Based on the information obtained during the SCAF, specific stimulus control intervention recommendations should be made in Session 2.

Stimulus control interventions should be individualized for the client. As such, on the following page is a list of possible stimulus control interventions that could be used if particular settings, tools, or presence of others is endorsed. This list is not exhaustive, and therapists and supervisors should feel free to come up with additional interventions. However, two principles should be adhered to when choosing and presenting such interventions so that they are theoretically consistent with AEBT-T:

1. Stimulus control interventions are done to make pulling more effortful, difficult, and problematic. This may result in the prevention of the pulling. For the purposes of AEBT-T, stimulus control techniques should not be done to prevent or avoid the emergence of uncomfortable urges, feelings, or thoughts. Such strategies are counterproductive to the AEBT-T model.

2. The stimulus control interventions should be simple, easy to implement, and, when possible, not socially disruptive.

Stimulus Control Intervention Recommendations

Setting	Possible Intervention
Bathroom	1. Keep the bathroom door open 2. Remove bright lights from the bathroom 3. Use a timer to limit amount of time in the bathroom
Watching TV or Playing Video Games	1. Sit in the middle of a couch or on a chair with no armrests 2. On top of the television place a timer that you have to reset by getting up every 10 minutes (to increase effort to stop and start pulling) 3. Hold a furry object or stress ball in your hands
Reading	1. Sit in the middle of a couch or on a chair with no armrests 2. Hold book with both hands 3. Hold a furry object or stress ball in one hand and the book in the other
Bedroom	1. Keep the bedroom door open 2. Lie in bed only when you're ready to sleep 3. Remove chairs with armrests
Use of Tweezers, Needles, Safety Pins, or Sharp Objects	1. Remove these objects from the house and from your purse
Use of Mirrors	1. Remove magnifying mirrors or lighted mirrors 2. Remove small mirrors from your purse 3. Cover mirrors in the bathroom 4. Limit use of mirror to 1 minute
Presence of Others	1. If pulling does not occur around others, try to recruit social-support people to be present in high-risk situations.

Chapter 5 | *Session 3: Valuing*

(Corresponds to chapter 3 of the workbook)

Materials Needed

■ How Has Fighting Your Urges Affected You form

■ Writing Your Epitaph form

Session Outline

■ Conduct weekly assessment of progress

■ Inquire about any reactions to material from previous session

■ Review homework

■ Discuss values

■ Assign homework

Completion of Assessment Measures

As in every session, the client should return or complete an assessment to gauge progress. This progress (or lack of it) and the client's reactions should be discussed. Help the client plot assessment data on the graph provided in the workbook.

Review of Previous Material

Ask the client to share her thoughts on and reactions to the topics discussed in Session 2.

Homework Review

Praise the client for engaging in the self-monitoring process, using the competing response, and implementing the stimulus control procedures as outlined in the previous session. Highlight the importance of continued monitoring and practice of the competing response and stimulus control procedures identified in Session 2. Plot the self-monitoring data on the daily graph (in the workbook) to examine fluctuations in pulling. Discuss any patterns and trends in the data, and ask the client why she thinks certain trends in the pulling may have developed (e.g., why do you think you pulled so often that day?). With the aid of the completed Monitoring Your Urge Form, ask the client to comment on what happened to her thoughts, urges, and feelings about pulling when using the competing response. Be sure to note the answers to these questions as client responses may become useful information in later sessions. Remind the client that she is only gathering information on her urges, and they are not to be addressed at this point in therapy.

If the client did not comply with the homework or refused to or was unable to use the competing response or stimulus control procedures, explore barriers to compliance, stress the importance of compliance, and formulate a plan to assure success with future assignments.

Valuing

The purpose of the valuing component is to link subsequent work to something bigger than simply decreasing the hair pulling. The client has likely come to therapy to reduce her pulling, and this is likely important to her because pulling has gotten in the way of accomplishing more important things. For the client, stopping the pulling is usually about getting back into important areas of her life. Many people with TTM have restricted social lives or have allowed their pulling to take time away from the things that are important to them. Values link the therapy to these ends.

Values are things that are important to a person, thus are things that the client would be willing to work toward in the face of uncomfortable private experiences. Values are different than goals in that goals are short term and temporary. Thus, stopping hair pulling is a goal and not a value. Being a good mother is a value. Goals can be steps toward enacting values, but values can never be fully achieved. When discussing values with the client, recognize that values can be easily translated into goals toward which the client is willing to direct her behavior. The therapist might say something to the client such as the following:

> *I know you probably came in here wanting my help to stop your pulling, and I want that too, but I think we both need to realize that stopping pulling isn't just about growing your hair out, it is about something much bigger. It is about getting your life back. It is about doing all those things that you have been waiting for. So we will work together on stopping the pulling, but we need to be aware that these struggles are larger than pulling.*

Work with the client on an assessment of her values, goals, and actions, and barriers that stand in the way of pursuing these values. Refer the client to the How Has Fighting Your Urges Affected You form in the workbook and ask the client to determine which of the areas in her life are affected by attempts to manage the urges. The client is free to list as many or as few areas as she feels are necessary. Briefly review areas that are not included in the values assessment to help the client notice all the areas that are important to her but she is prevented from pursuing because of her attempting to control the urges. The overall function of this form is to help the client see what is important to her and how her fights against the urges have held her back from living a life that she wants. This information will become useful in later sessions, when you offer the idea that giving up on this fight against the urges might allow her to live a more valued life.

Another way to help the client determine her values is to ask her what she would want written on her tombstone. The client can write down her thoughts on the Writing Your Epitaph form in Chapter 3 of the workbook. It is likely that she will not write that she wants to control her pulling, but rather something about being a good family member or changing something in the world. Talk with the client about how her struggles with her urges to pull have taken her away from these values. Ask her if she thinks it might be worth working through the difficulty of treatment to get to the point where she no longer pulls and pursues those things that are important to her.

Another way to address this is to ask the client how she wants to see herself in 5, 10, or 20 years.

Summarizing Values

At the end of the session discuss with the client the consequences of becoming focused on where she is in therapy to the exclusion of fully participating in treatment. This is a relatively simple topic and can be presented in many ways. The therapist may say something such as the following:

> *The point of many activities is the activity itself, not the end result. Take rock climbing, for example. The point really isn't to get to the top of the rock—if that were the case I am sure that there are easier ways to do that than climb the face. It is the process of climbing that is the point of the activity. Therapy is also like that. Even if we could magically make trichotillomania go away, I am not sure we would want to. The process of working through this issue is an important step in your life. Enjoy the process of therapy, and don't miss it.*

This description may be useful throughout the course of therapy, particularly when the client feels she is not making progress or is evaluating herself on the basis of a "struggle" with intense urges to pull. At these times, you can suggest to the client that she is focusing too much on getting to the top of the climb rather than the climbing itself.

✎ Instruct the client to continue to monitor hair-pulling episodes and reactions to the urges to pull over the course of the next week (using the TTM Self-Monitoring and Monitoring Your Urge forms), engage in the chosen competing response, and implement stimulus control procedures.

✎ Ask the client to spend time considering the areas of her life that she wants to pursue and the ways in which pulling and struggling with her urges to pull have taken her away from these areas.

Chapter 6 | *Session 4: Can Urges Be Controlled?*

(Corresponds to chapter 4 of the workbook)

There are no materials needed for this session.

Session Outline

- Conduct weekly assessment of progress

- Inquire about any reactions to material from previous session

- Review homework

- Continue discussion of barriers to valued goals

- Introduce concept of long-term effects of control

- Assign homework

Completion of Assessment Measures

As in every session, the client should return or complete an assessment to gauge progress. This progress (or lack of it) and the client's reactions should be discussed. Help the client plot assessment data on the graph provided in the workbook.

Review of Previous Material

Ask the client to share her thoughts on and reactions to the topics discussed in Session 3.

Homework Review

Praise the client for engaging in the self-monitoring and urge-monitoring processes. Review and troubleshoot the implementation of the HRT and stimulus control procedures, and point out the importance of continued monitoring and use of competing responses and stimulus control procedures. Plot the self-monitoring data on the daily graph (in the workbook) to examine fluctuations in pulling. Discuss patterns and trends in the data, and ask the client why she thinks certain trends in the pulling may have developed (e.g., "why do you think you pulled so often that day?").

Continue Discussing the Barriers to Pursuing Values

Resume the discussion from Session 3 about the barriers that seem to stand in the way of the client engaging in actions that are meaningful to her. If the client does not specifically bring up trying to control her urges and hair pulling as a barrier, ask her what role, if any, these play in her values and goals. Discussion of how the hair pulling interferes with the client's values will be addressed in the following section. Many clients may state that the hair pulling is the actual barrier to the accomplishment of their goals, but further questioning will show that it is the emotional reactions to pulling and an unwillingness to maintain contact with unpleasant private experiences typically alleviated by pulling that are the true barriers to moving in a valued-life direction. This information will be elaborated on in the next section.

Long-Term Utility of Control

In this phase of the program, help the client see her struggle with her urges and other private experiences more clearly. Clarify whether avoiding settings that produce urges or engaging in efforts to reduce urges works in the long-run. Typically, these strategies reduce urges to pull for minutes or hours, but they do not work for meaningful amounts of time. The urge will often reappear very shortly. Remembering the data from Chapter 1—it is not the urge that is the problem, but the way that the client responds to the urge. The feeling itself is not the issue; it is reducing the feeling through pulling or other means that is the problem. Efforts to reduce or control the urges, thoughts, or emotions surrounding pulling make sense to the client because they work in the short term. The long-term adverse effects are not noted because they are distally related to the pulling. The client needs to become aware of this situation.

Discuss the following areas of the client's change agenda: 1) what does the client do to control her urges to pull, thoughts preceding pulling, or negative emotions surrounding pulling (e.g., pulls, avoids situation that make her want to pull, avoids stressful situations, rubs cream on her head, etc.); 2) how well does this control strategy work in the short term (usually works very well); 3) how well does this work in the long term, such as for days and weeks (i.e., does the urge return later?); 4) what are the costs of these strategies (e.g., loss of hair, loss of time, emotional toll); and 5) is the struggle with the urge becoming larger or smaller (usually people report larger). The client's completed Monitoring Your Urge forms from the first 3 weeks of treatment are useful in facilitating this discussion.

The purpose of this discussion is to help the client see how damaging the control agenda can become. One of the major points that a therapist should note when working with persons with TTM is that pulling one's hair reduces aversive private events or increases feelings of pleasure in the short term, but it is generally ineffective and costly in the long term.

Case Vignette

Therapist: You've been struggling with pulling for a long time, but I'll bet there's a part of you that worries about giving it up.

Client: Yeah, I've been doing it for so long, it's like my hair is always there for me.

Therapist: How do you mean, "it's always there for you?"

Client: Well, whenever I feel upset or bored, or get that awful urge to pull, pulling is what takes care of it.

Therapist: So would it be fair to say that pulling helps you deal with that unpleasant stuff?

Client: Yeah, that would be fair.

Therapist: What else have you tried to deal with that mental stuff?

Client: Well, I've tried all kinds of self-help books, I've tried ignoring the emotions, I've tried relaxing, I've tried tying a string around my finger to remind myself not to pull, everything.

Therapist: Pulling?

Client: Yep, that too . . . and I guess coming here too.

Therapist: How have these things worked for you?

Client: Well, pulling gets rid of the urges and makes me forget about my stress for a little while.

Therapist: Does it last?

Client: I guess not.

Therapist: Tell me about how long you can keep the urge away. I mean, if you really tried hard.

Client: I can only keep it away for a couple minutes. I see something or think of something and it is back.

Therapist: It is almost as if the more you try, the bigger it gets.

Client: Yes.

Therapist: So short term you are pretty good at it, but long term is a different issue. The urge always comes back. If you pull often one night and the urge is completely gone, it will be back the next night, right?

Client: Yes, there is never a day I go without the urge.

Therapist: But you work hard at controlling it.

Client: It is like a full-time job—worse actually, you get breaks from full-time jobs.

Therapist: Then let's look at this urge over the years. Do you find that it is getting bigger or smaller?

Client: It's getting bigger.

Therapist: Okay, we are on to something here. This urge can only be controlled for minutes and hours, not long meaningful periods of time like days and weeks, and it seems to be getting bigger over time, not smaller. This is good information. We need to know how this works. We also need to look at the costs of trying to control these urges. The basic reason you pull is to reduce this urge that you have to pull your hair. The basic reason you avoid stressful situations is because they will make you have the urge. You skip lots of activities because it makes you want to pull. How much of your life is dedicated to controlling these urges to pull?

Client: Most of it actually. It is sort of sad.

Therapist: Let me wrap this up for you a little. You spend most of your time trying to control your urges, but they never go away for any meaningful periods of time. Actually, they are getting stronger every year. Finally, all the things that you are doing to control these urges are affecting your life in very significant detrimental ways. It sounds like this is a pretty bad setup. You are playing a rigged game. Maybe the reason you can't control these urges is that they are not controllable. It is not that you have not tried hard enough; it's because nothing you can do will work. Maybe it's time you stopped hurting yourself.

Client: What? And just live with this urge?

Therapist: Let's face it. You are living with it now. You can live with it and pull and fight, or live with it without the pulling and fighting. Remember, you have been fighting with it and it has been getting stronger, not weaker.

Continue with this discussion until the client begins to see that her attempts at controlling urges to pull are not effective in the long run and are actually more damaging than useful. If the client does not agree, don't push it. Send the client home with homework of trying everything she can to keep her urges under control and then discuss how effective it was at the next session. The client will not be able to do this because that is not how urges work. If the client were able to control urges to pull hair she would have done it already. If the client is on board with this conceptualization, you may move on. To facilitate further understanding of this paradoxical situation, the following metaphor can be used.

The goal of this metaphor is to help the client gain willingness to drop her old control agenda.

Two-Games Metaphor

Therapist: Let me give you an example of what I think has been going on, and you can tell me what you think. You have been playing a tennis match for most of your life, against your urges, thoughts, and emotions surrounding pulling. When your urges are bad, you start to pull to keep them under control. When you go for a couple hours or a day without urges to pull, you think you're winning. Except there is something that is really unfair about this match: you're playing it against the best professional player on the planet. So you don't really do too well. You win a game here and there, but really you keep losing set after set, match after match. The urge just keeps coming back. Your opponent is way better than you, you're having a hard time beating her, and you're getting tired of trying. In a way the match is fair. It follows the usual rules of a tennis match, but it is unfair in that you can't win. Your opponent is the best! This must be frustrating, because if you could win the match, the urges to pull would stop. If you could only win the match, you could lay down the racquet and go and do all those things you have been missing, such as dating, swimming, finding a new job, etc. Does this seem like your situation?

Client: Yes. So what do I do? That is why I am here. How do I control this urge to pull?

Therapist: I think you have tried beating it, haven't you?

Client: Sure I have tried lots of things—books, Web sites, holding a ball; I even worked with a therapist to learn how to relax. It worked for a while, but the urges got too strong.

Therapist: That's right, and if your pulling didn't involve any of those urges, emotions, or thoughts about pulling, those things may have been enough. However, in the game of urges, all the books, Web sites, and relaxation still can't beat the best.

Client: So, what do you suggest?

Therapist: Here is my offer. There is another game of tennis over here that most people do not pay attention to. It is similar to the first game in some ways, but also different in other very important ways. To begin with, this game is fair. It is you playing against someone who is about as good as you. Therefore, the more you put into it, the more you generally get out of it. Most importantly, you're not playing for whether or not you have urges; you're playing for the quality of your life. Instead of getting your urges, thoughts, or emotions under control before you move forward, what if we just started moving forward? What if your job wasn't to win the first tennis match, but to walk away from the match and play a different match where you play for your values?

Client: Are you saying that we are not going to work on my urges?

Therapist: Listen very carefully. We are definitely not going to do anything that your mind expects with these urges. We are going to do something radically different. Desperate times call for desperate measures. It will be difficult because you will be tempted to look over there and play your old tennis match. I mean, you've been playing for a long time, maybe even since your pulling started. But, tell me if it isn't true, that in order to play Game 1 you have to stop doing the other stuff, the stuff that makes your life whole.

Client: Sure. When I am pulling I am not doing other things. I am usually up in the bathroom with my tweezers, by myself.

Therapist: Okay, are you willing to take a look at the idea that you don't need to win the match with your urges before you start doing other things, the really important things to you?

Client: Let's give it a try.

Likely, the client will try to make sense of the metaphor or make a new rule out of it (e.g., "So if I just stop trying to control the urge, then it will go away"). This is common. This is a very different approach to the problem, and the client may have a difficult time understanding at first. If the client does try to create a new rule about how to control the urge, it can be helpful to say something like the following:

Maybe, but it sounds to me like you may have just started playing tennis with your urges again. Could that be the case? I know this will be difficult, but for now, I'd like you to keep an open mind about the things we discuss. Try not to figure it out all at once.

Refer back to the two-games metaphor when the client is trying to control her urges instead of doing things that are important to her.

Homework

✎ Ask the client to take a half-sheet of paper (or use the form provided in the workbook) and write down a private event that she attempts to control through pulling (e.g., the urge, a thought about unevenness in the hair, etc.). Instruct the client to fold the paper in half three times and place it between her foot and shoe and keep it there for the course of the week. Do not elaborate on the exercise. Explain to the client that you will discuss the purpose of this experiment at the next session.

✎ The client should continue monitoring hair-pulling episodes over the course of the next week using the TTM Self-Monitoring Form.

✎ The client should continue to use the chosen competing response and implement stimulus control procedures.

Chapter 7 | *Session 5: Acceptance*

(Corresponds to chapter 5 of the workbook)

Materials Needed

■ Behavioral Commitment Worksheet and Instructions

Session Outline

■ Conduct weekly assessment of progress

■ Inquire about any reactions to material from previous session

■ Review homework

■ Introduce willingness as an alternative to trying to control urges to pull

■ Introduce and establish behavioral commitments

■ Assign homework

Completion of Assessment Measures

As in every session, the client should return or complete an assessment to gauge progress. This progress (or lack of it) and the client's reactions should be discussed. Help the client plot assessment data on the graph provided in the workbook.

Review of Previous Material

Ask the client to share her thoughts on and reactions to the topics discussed in Session 4.

Homework Review

Praise the client for engaging in the self-monitoring process. Review and troubleshoot implementation of the HRT and stimulus control procedures, and point out the importance of continued monitoring and use of competing-responses and stimulus control procedures. Plot the self-monitoring data on the daily graph (in the workbook) to examine fluctuations in pulling. Discuss patterns and trends in the data, and ask the client why she thinks certain trends in the pulling may have developed.

If the client was given the assignment to try to prevent the urges (because she still believed it was possible after the last session), review her efforts and discuss any experiences or insights she may have encountered. When discussing the homework, it is possible that the client will have seen new things about her urges and want advice on how to fix the problem. These new insights could include certain times when and places where pulling is common, certain thoughts that precede pulling, and feelings that coexist with pulling. Avoid giving the client any new urge control strategies and help the client see that the old control strategies have not worked and that she may easily be led to use them.

Accepting Private Events (Willingness)

During this session, work with the client on an alternative way of responding to hair-pulling urges, pulling-related cognitions, and emotions that have commonly led to pulling: acceptance of these experiences. In the previous session the client should have noticed that her strategies to control private events have been largely unsuccessful in the long term and possibly quite costly.

Case Vignette

Therapist: I want to talk about Game 1 from last week and how people get trapped in it. There is a certain assumption in society that if you don't like something, there is a way to change it. All and all, that is pretty fair to say, because we can change most things we don't like. For example, if it is cold in the room, you can turn up the heat; if you don't like your clothes, you can get new ones, etc. But this has been applied to many additional situations. For example, there are many ads on television for different pharmaceuticals for all sorts of "problems" such as anxiety, depression, sleep, and sexual urges. I am not saying that these are bad things—they have helped a lot of people—but they are very much Game 1-type strategies. If you are feeling depressed, instead of finding things you enjoy, you can "take a pill"; if you are not feeling sexually attracted to your husband, you can "take a pill," instead of doing romantic things. We have gotten to this place where if our emotions are not at a certain "acceptable" level we must change that before we can do anything. This is Game 1-fighting the unpleasant stuff that shows up inside our own skin.

Client: But isn't it hard to be active when you are depressed? I know that is how I am.

Therapist: Absolutely. But in there is the belief that depression must be removed before you can get active. That is the message that society teaches you. How would this apply to hair pulling?

Client: It has to do with urges. Probably something like, "My urges have to decrease before I can stop pulling."

The notion that trying to suppress or otherwise placate urges, emotions, or cognitions related to hair pulling is actually counterproductive can be strengthened through the use of the following two metaphors:

Therapist: I want to spend a little more time on this "control" thing. It seems as though we should be able to control the stuff the shows up in our bodies, right? It seems like we should be able to control what we think and the feelings that we have. I mean, that is what you have been doing with your urges to pull. Let's do an exercise. I want you to put your hand to your head [or wherever she pulls from] and feel one of your favorite pulling areas. Now I have one simple task: just don't get an urge to pull. That is it. [*While the client does this, say things that make it more likely that she will get an urge, such as talking about the types of hairs that she enjoys pulling.*] How did that work?

Client: Duh! I have the urge now and I will probably want to pull more at home tonight.

Therapist: Okay. That was a little difficult. Let's try a thought. For the next minute I want you to not think about your favorite hairs that you pull. Don't think about the ones with big roots, that are thicker than the others, etc. [*Continue to give little reminders to keep the client thinking about her favorite hairs.*] Okay. How did that work?

Client: This is totally unfair. It is impossible and you are making me want to pull.

Therapist: Just to be fair, I am not doing anything that your mind is not already doing. Your mind does this all day long. It tries to avoid the urges and gets pulled into thinking about the "good" hairs. Are you sensing what this struggle does to you? Now, let's try something different. Please don't touch that tissue box [or another object in the room]. I want to see if you can go a whole minute without doing that.

Client: That's simple. What an odd request.

Therapist: But the task is exactly the same; just don't do one simple thing. Don't have an urge, think about good hairs, or touch something. Notice that the first two have to do with thoughts and feelings and the last one is a thing you do. They are different. They work under different rules. You have been applying outside-the-body rules to thoughts and feelings. They don't work there. The outside world works differently than the inside world.

At this point it is useful to process the "paper in shoe" exercise assigned at the end of Session 4. In the exercise, the tactile sensations generated by the paper in the shoe should be equated to the private event (written on the paper) for which the client uses pulling to control. The exercise has multiple purposes. The first is to demonstrate to the client how the "urge" will show up at random—it will be there at times and it will be gone at times—it is not under the client's control. Likewise, it also demonstrates to the client that if she starts interacting with the "urge" by thinking about it, shifting her foot around, trying not to notice it, etc., then it will get more noticeable and she will be less involved in her ongoing life. Through this physical metaphor, the client should see that the more one interacts with an internal sensation, the more salient it becomes. She should also see that the sensations will come and go naturally, but only if left alone. If interacted with, they will remain present.

Case Vignette

Therapist: So, last week, I had you put the paper in your shoe. I'm sure that seemed a bit odd. How did it go for you?

Client: You're right, it was a bit weird, but I did it. You know what? It drove me crazy for the first day or so. I was always adjusting my shoe, and always moving the paper around.

Therapist: So you kept getting involved with the paper and kept noticing it at first. Then what happened?

Client: Eventually, I just kind of forgot about it, and went about my day.

Therapist: What happened to the sensations created by the paper? Were they always there?

Client: No, sometimes they were there, sometimes they went away. A lot of it had to do with how I moved my foot. If I moved it the right way, the sensations showed up.

Therapist: So sometimes they were there, sometimes they weren't. Kind of like your urges. What happened when you started playing with the paper, or moving your foot around to get rid of the sensations? Did you notice the sensations at those times?

Client: Definitely.

Therapist: So when you tried to get rid of the sensations they were there, and when you left them alone and did other things, sometimes they were there and sometimes they weren't?

Client: Yep.

Therapist: I wonder if your urges [or whatever was written on the paper] to pull do the same thing?

Most of the work in this session has been about helping the client to see that the urge is incredibly difficult, if not impossible, to control. At this point it is hoped that the client's dedication to controlling it has lessened, and she sees that that Game 1 in the two-games metaphor is unfair and that Game 2 seems like an interesting second option. Offer *acceptance* of these private experiences to pull as an alternate option to pulling as a means of gaining control of her life.

Acceptance of private events is a behavioral term that means not engaging in actions to remove or decrease certain private events. It involves letting them be there as they are and not fighting with them in any way. It is a choice. It is different from tolerating: it is willfully inviting the unwanted private experiences in the same way one would let a less desirable family member stay as a houseguest. Through AEBT-T the client is taught to let her urges and other pulling-related private events occur and to just observe them. This concept is sometimes difficult to grasp. In the simplest terms, the basis for using acceptance in AEBT-T is that **urges can't be controlled, so we need to make room for them in our lives**. We can either have them, resent them every day, and try to get rid of them, or we can willfully invite them in. This next metaphor is a way to present willfully inviting them in and not getting pulled into fighting with them.

Case Vignette

Therapist: Let's go back to those two games I was talking about, the tennis match with your urges, and the other game you were playing for the quality of your life. Let's pretend that you have agreed to stop playing Game 1 and will totally focus on the second game. How well do you think you would do at Game 2 if you spent part of that game watching the best player from Game 1 play someone else while you were supposed to be playing in Game 2?

Client: Well obviously not very well. You can't be distracted from the game you're playing and expect to have a decent chance of winning.

Therapist: Yes. In order to do this you really have to completely give up on Game 1. Any time that you get dragged into it is time and effort taken away from the one you have a fair shot at. It will be difficult. You will want to get involved in the other game; you will be curious what the current score is. There might even be moments when you are doing surprisingly well working on Game 1 and want to start playing it a little. Watch out! That might just be the best player trying to pull you into playing Game 1 again. This is an all-or-nothing thing. You can't try it, just like you can't try jumping off a diving board. You either do it or not. If you want to try Game 2, you have to give up Game 1 completely.

Acceptance of Urges versus Acceptance of Non-valued Behavior

The purpose of therapy to this point has been twofold. The first phase of treatment was designed to teach the client a strategy to control pulling, and the second involved teaching the client to be willing to experience unpleasant thoughts, images, urges, or emotions involved in pulling. To provide an adequate assimilation of both phases, it must be clear why an apparent shift is occurring. If the client views HRT as an attempt to control the urge to pull rather than the pulling itself, she will become confused, as it contradicts the principles of ACT. To eliminate this issue, some version of the following statement should be made.

> *Up to this point, we have spent some time discussing control strategies for actual pulling, and recently we have focused on learning to be willing to accept some private events. However, at no point during the course of therapy did we ever discuss being accepting of the actual pulling. You may have thought that this was kind of strange, but we did this for a reason. Since our second session together we have been engaging in HRT and stimulus control to manage your pulling and have been reviewing your progress in using these procedures successfully. These strategies can be useful to stop doing actual behaviors that don't allow you to accomplish your valued goals. You may have no-*

ticed already that when you stop pulling, the urges might come up, and that's why we are working on being willing to have those experiences. So, what we have done is given you HRT and stimulus control to stop the pulling and tried to prepare you for a lot of the private "stuff" you've tried to control through pulling. At this point, we're going to keep using HRT and stimulus control procedures to stop the pulling, but we're also going to start using them as tools to help you practice being more accepting or willing to experience the private events that in the past have led to more pulling.

Behavioral Commitments

At this point, and through the end of treatment, work with the client to seek opportunities to pursue valued activities over controlling her urges to pull. A contrast should be created between behavior that is in the service of controlling private events and that following her values. Controlling urges to pull usually takes the client away from what is important to her. For example, time spent pulling in the bathroom is time away from friends and family. Similarly, avoiding social events because they might increase anxiety or the urge to pull is more about regulation of private events rather than doing what is really important to her. Following her values will allow her opportunities to encounter the reinforcing properties of the skills being taught in the therapy. These exercises are called "behavioral commitment exercises."

There are some general parameters to doing behavioral commitment exercises. First, behavioral commitment exercises should be presented as opportunities to follow her values instead of controlling her urges to pull. Work with the client to determine steps she can make toward enacting her values that had been avoided because of their effects on her urges to pull. This process can involve many types of activities, such as spending less time pulling and more time with her family, attending events she would usually avoid because of urges or the results of her pulling, not pulling while watching television so that she is more present with her family or the television show, and many others. The Behavioral Commitment Worksheet in Chapter 5 of the workbook can be used to help the client develop her exercises. She should choose a situation where she will have success. It is more important that the exercise be a success rather than being large. The client can be reminded to use HRT and stimulus control to help stop the pulling during the behavioral commitment exercise. It is important to note that at times this may involve setting aside a prescribed stimulus-control intervention for the period of the exercise.

The second parameter of doing a behavioral commitment exercise is that success is determined by whether the prescribed task is completed, not by the levels of urges or some other private event the client experiences during the task. Thus, the client could experience a Subjective Units of Discomfort (SUDS) rating of 100 with no reduction during the behavioral commitment exercise, but if the person completed the exercise as described it would be considered a success. The client is committing to engaging in a valued activity that will likely create some urges to pull for a specified period of time or over the course of a specified activity. There is no concern for the private events experienced during the activity.

Third, completing these exercises is not about tolerating or "toughing out" the urges to pull for a specified period of time. The client should agree to be completely open to what shows up during the exercise. Success in this area is not based on whether private events do or do not show up. Rather, success is based on how willing the client is to experience what shows up. Thus, if the client agrees to get ready in the washroom without pulling (so that she can be with her partner sooner), she is agreeing to getting ready without fighting any particular feelings that show up. If none show up, then it was only important that she was open to the possibility of them showing up.

This phase is really about helping the client get back into her life. She will gradually start doing the things that she has been avoiding, and will have opportunities to practice the work that has been taught in session. Most clients get pulled back into how strong the urge is during the exercise; the therapist will need to help reorient the client to the overall function of behavioral commitment exercises: to do what is important to her rather than alter her urge to pull.

Homework

✎ The client should continue to monitor hair-pulling episodes over the course of the next week using the TTM Self-Monitoring Form, engage in the chosen competing response, and implement stimulus control procedures.

✎ The client should choose a behavioral commitment exercise to practice each day over the course of the next week for an agreed-upon period of time.

Chapter 8

Sessions 6 & 7: Defusion from the Literal Meaning of Language: You Are Not Your Urges

(Corresponds to chapter 6 of the workbook)

There are no materials needed for this session.

Session Outline

- Conduct weekly assessment of progress

- Inquire about any reactions to material from the previous session

- Review homework

- Discuss defusion of language

- Conduct various exercises to show the client what private events really are—just private events

- Assign homework

    Sessions 6 and 7 are combined into one chapter because both sessions focus on the topics of defusion. These processes can be addressed in a number of ways. This chapter includes 10 different exercises aimed at addressing these processes in TTM. They need not all be used, but should be used as needed to help the client view her thoughts, urges, and emotions as a nonliteral, ongoing process that is separate from her.

Completion of Assessment Measures

As in every session, the client should return or complete an assessment to gauge progress. This progress (or lack of it) and the client's reactions should be discussed. Help the client plot assessment data on the graph provided in the workbook.

Review of Previous Material

Ask the client to share her thoughts on and reactions to the topics discussed in the previous weeks.

Homework Review

Praise the client for engaging in the self-monitoring process. Review and troubleshoot the implementation of the HRT and stimulus control procedures, and point out the importance of continued monitoring and use of competing responses and stimulus control procedures. Plot the self-monitoring data on the daily graph (in the workbook) to examine fluctuations in pulling. Discuss patterns and trends in the data, and ask the client why she thinks certain trends in the pulling may have developed. Review behavioral commitment exercises.

Defusion of Language

As a normal part of language development, we become fused with our language. In other words, we start reacting to language as if the words were as real or true as the object or event they represent. This is called "cognitive fusion," and it is particularly problematic in TTM, as clients see their urges, anxieties, and cognitions as true events that must be acted upon. To counter this process, ACT uses defusion, which involves creating a therapeutic context that breaks down the literality of verbal processes. The purpose of defusion exercises is not to change the client's thinking from something that is illogical to something that is logical. Rather, it is to change the context of language from something that supports private events as literal events to something that supports private events as something to simply be experienced. Defusion helps the client to see private events for what they are, not for what they present themselves to be. An example of this could be when a person tries to resist hair pulling and therefore feels great tension and says privately, "If I don't pull my hair I will go crazy." The urge is only a feeling and the thought "If I don't pull my hair I will go crazy" is only a thought. Both are language based and have functional properties in certain contexts, specifically those contexts that reinforce and otherwise support the literality of language. When the context supporting non-literality is created, the functional impact of these private events on pulling should diminish.

Defusion exercises are limitless because there are many ways a therapist can help the client respond to thoughts less literally. Although there are many good examples in other books on ACT, a useful approach to pulling-related private events is provided here. This session could start out with a discussion about the need for defusion.

Case Vignette

Therapist: I want to talk about your thoughts, emotions, and urges that lead you into hair pulling. I am not interested in whether these things make sense or if they are accurate or not. I want to talk about the way in which you work with them. When you are pulling hair, what are you usually thinking? What are you usually feeling?

Client: I start out thinking that that I probably should not even start, but then I will see or feel a hair that really needs to be pulled out. I will usually start pulling and talking to myself about which hairs are the good ones and where I should pull. There is always the end part where I criticize myself for pulling and feel bad about what I've been doing.

Therapist: After it starts, do you notice yourself thinking about your pulling while you are doing it, or does it just feel natural?

Client: After it starts, I just do it.

Therapist: Right, most people are not really aware that they are thinking. We just go along day and night with our minds jabbering at us. Our minds talk, describe, criticize, and analyze all day long. This process is really useful when you are at a grocery store looking for ingredients for soup, but this same process really gets in the way when you are looking for good hairs to pull, or when you are trying to talk yourself out of pulling. *Your mind is not always your friend.*

Client: So what do I do with it?

Therapist: The first step is to notice that your mind is always talking to you. Minds are like colored sunglasses that you always wear. You look through them so much that 99% of the time you don't even know you are wearing them. You don't know your mind is having a say about everything that happens, everything you see.

One part of defusion is the ability to see that a person has thoughts that are separate from herself and that thoughts and feelings affect the way we experience the world. To help the client see that her mind is always active, she can participate in the following exercise in session. The exercise should be conducted slowly, while you use a calm tone of voice.

Exercise—Being Present

I would like you to do a little exercise with me. It will involve closing your eyes, listening, and following along with what I say. I am not trying to hypnotize you or make you relax. If you get relaxed, that is fine, but it is not my goal. My goal is to help you become more aware that you are thinking.

Close your eyes or stare at a blank spot on the wall. I don't need you to respond—just listen.

I want you to pay attention to your breathing. Pay attention to what each breath feels like as it comes in and what it feels like as it goes back out. Notice that there is a temperature difference as it comes back out. Notice what your belly feels like as it lowers and rises. Notice who is noticing these things. It is you.

Now listen to the different sounds that are in the room. There are the loud, obvious ones like the fan in the computer, but there are subtler ones, like the sounds in the hall or outside. See if you can't notice those. As you listen to these sounds, notice who is hearing them.

Here is the real exercise. I want you to watch the thoughts that show up in your mind. Imagine you are sitting in a theater looking at a big, empty stage. The play starts, but instead of actors coming out, your thoughts walk out. Just pay attention to what shows up in front of you as if you were watching a play. See your thoughts out on the stage. There will be some thoughts or feelings that you don't like, that you might want to get rid of. Just notice that urge to get rid of them and continue watching your thoughts on the stage. [Let the client do this for a couple minutes and gently remind her to continue with the exercise.]

If you are having the thought, "I am not sure what it is I am supposed to be doing," then put that one on the stage. Actors always come and go in plays, so as new thoughts show up, they should go on stage, just as new actors would. When thoughts go, they will leave the stage, just as actors will in a real play.

There will be moments when you are no longer doing the exercise and you are only thinking. I call that "buying into a thought." Just notice the difference between that time and watching thoughts on the stage. If that happens, gently bring yourself back to the exercise and get it going again.

Help the client see that her mind does not stop, that it always has something to say. It is likely that she bought into a thought about a particularly difficult topic, such as her hair pulling. Talk to the client about how the mind grabs on to certain topics. It can be helpful to show this by starting a sentence and showing her that the mind will finish it. For example, say, "Mary had a little . . . " or "Blonds have more . . . " The client's mind will automatically finish these statements. Help normalize this for the client. This is just what minds do. Similarly, she can't help that thoughts about pulling are going to show when she is in certain situations, such as in the bathroom. Thus, the question is not how do we stop this process, but how can we notice it and respond to it for what it is. The following metaphor can help demonstrate this point.

Tree-on-the-Road Metaphor

It is sort of like the following two scenarios. In the first, you're going to a really important meeting (your values), and the fastest way to get there is on this back road. As you drive down the road, you come to a point where a large tree has fallen across it. You would like to keep going, but the tree is in the way. You don't have a saw or a way to tow it out of the way, so you must stop, and you can't continue until the tree is out of the way. It is a real problem, and one you must solve. Often, this is how we treat our urges to pull hair—when they get in the way we stop what we're doing and drag it out of the way. But is this really the best approach? Are the urges to pull really like trees in the road? Can we really not continue toward our values until the urges are removed?

Consider a second scenario. You are driving down the same road, but are waved down by a group of laughing teenagers who say, "You can't keep going because a large tree has fallen over the road." Now, the teenagers may be telling the truth or may simply be having some fun with an out-of-towner. Although you can't see the tree for yourself, you have a choice, you can keep going with this warning in your head, or you can turn around as though there really is a tree up ahead. What if urges are like warnings, but not the actual tree? Could you keep going in your valued direction, even in the presence of those urges? How do you treat you urges to pull hair? As real trees that are on the road or as warnings? Remember, trees are really in the way; warnings are not the actual thing you are being warned about.

Choice

When it comes to pulling, clients often feel they don't have a choice in pulling. The urges are strong and cognitions that sometimes lead to pulling seem accurate in the pulling moment. Still, the client does have a choice. To make that choice clear, and to show where the control over pulling lies, the following exercise is useful.

Stand in front of the client and ask her to use any words, cravings, urges, or emotions to get you to walk. The only rule is that the client cannot physically touch you. Only words, cravings, urges, or emotions can be used. Regardless of what the client says, do not move. Clients usually start by saying, "walk." When you don't move, she may say something like "pick up your right foot, and place it in front of you." When you still don't move, the client may try a number of other things. Eventually, the client just sits there or says that she "can't make you move." At this point, begin a discussion on the nature of thoughts, emotions, or urges, paying specific attention to the fact that they are not a physical entity and, as such, cannot exert physical force on an object. Then, revisit with the client how much control she thinks words, urges, cravings, or emotions actually have over behavior. It is then useful to point out that even though the urges, thoughts, or emotions make it feel like the client has no choice in whether to pull, ultimately, it is the choice of the client whether she pulls. In any instance where the pulling is about to occur, the client should understand that she has a choice. An attempt should be made to relate the exercise back to the client's pulling experience.

Exercise—Acting without Reasons

In this exercise, called "acting without reasons," the client is shown that she can choose to stop pulling rather than trying to talk herself into stopping. The function of this exercise is to help the client make choices without having to satisfy her mind that she is making the right one. It involves asking the client to think of reasons why she should not pull and then come up with counter-reasons for pulling. If she really works at it she will be able to come up with just about as many reasons to pull as those not to pull. Use this information to help her see that her mind will not let her work this problem out logically; not pulling is a matter of choice (a decision made without reasons). The following dialogue illustrates this.

Case Vignette

Therapist: We are going to do a little exercise to help you see how useful your mind is at helping you decide whether you should pull or not. Tell me about the last time you really struggled with whether you should pull or not and then ended up giving in.

Client: Last night is a good example. I was getting ready to go to sleep, I saw that there were a couple of odd hairs, and the urge to pull them just shot up. I thought that I had been doing really well with my pulling—my hair is coming in—but I really wanted to pull those hairs out. You know me, if I pull a couple, then I usually end up pulling a bunch. I knew that if I pulled that I would be mad at myself for giving in, but I knew that if I didn't, then I would have this urge all night and might not sleep well. I really struggled with what I should do.

Therapist: It sounds like it was hard for you to make a choice last night.

Client: I ended up pulling for only 5 minutes. That is really good for me.

Therapist: Good job keeping your pulling down. I want to talk about this struggle that you had over whether to pull or not. Let's come up with five good reasons that you should not pull.

Client: That's easy. 1) I will look better. 2) I will have more time. 3) I will not have to feel so bad about myself. 4) My mom will be off my back. 5) Finally, I will be able to do things like swimming, sports, and dating without worrying about my bald spots.

Therapist: Great job. Those are all very good reasons. Let's come up with some reasons to pull.

Client: Why would I want to do that?

Therapist: I am not saying you are going to follow them. I just want to show you the limits of your mind. I bet we can make a pretty good argument to pull. It is a little silly, but let's give it a try.

Client: 1) If I pull then I don't have to deal with the urge for a little while. 2) I do actually enjoy the pulling sometimes. 3) It is a part of my life that I am unsure about giving up. That is all I can think of.

Therapist: Make up some goofy ones, such as maybe a tweezers company will hire me to test their tweezers.

Client: Okay. Maybe pulling is actually good for your health and the doctors don't know it.

Therapist: Great. I bet we could come up with 100 more reasons for pulling and 100 against it, right? Maybe this is not a problem that we can figure out logically. You are a smart person and will be able to make a good argument for or against pulling. Have you ever watched politicians debate? They are generally pretty good at arguing both sides of an issue. You can do the same thing in your head. Therefore, pulling or not pulling may be a choice—an action done without reasons—rather than a decision—an action done for reasons.

Exercise—Playing with Urges in a Different Way

The content of this exercise is similar to that of defusion exercises described in other ACT books. It is often helpful to let people interact with their private events (thoughts, feelings, and bodily sensations) in a different, goofy way. Clients often take their thoughts about hair pulling and urges very seriously and literally. Exercises like these, in which the client interacts with her thoughts and urges to pull in a different way, lessen how literally these thoughts are experienced. These exercises can be started by having the client touch her head or think about pulling to induce the urge to pull. Feel free to make up other ways that one can interact with urges to pull. Here are some examples:

1. Have the client describe her urges to pull as being either a cat or a dog. Have her describe the breed, age, size, color, activity level, etc. Get her to talk about what the cat or dog (urge) is like. Finally, ask if there is anything about this animal that she can't take care of. Would she have this animal in her life if it needed a home? Would she adopt it?

2. Ask her to describe the urge as if it were a television commercial. What would it be an advertisement for? What would be taking place? What voices would be in it? You can tell the client to think of her urges or self-talk about pulling in this way when at home.

3. What would the urge be like as a television wrestler? What type of mask would it wear? What size would it be?

4. She can also imagine her urges to pull or thoughts about pulling as pop-up ads on her computer, an announcer at a baseball game, or a screaming child at a grocery store.

Exercise—Evaluation versus Description

This exercise focuses on helping the client experience her urges to pull and thoughts about pulling more as they actually are and less as what her mind tells her they are. In a factual way, urges are not dangerous things. No feeling is actually dangerous. It is the way we respond to them that can be dangerous. Pulling to get rid of the urge, avoiding social situations to prevent embarrassment, or avoiding relationships causes problems.

People sometimes seek out the very same feelings that they work so hard to avoid or eliminate. For example, some people ride roller coasters, but avoid a similar feeling of anxiety that comes along with meeting a new person. Strip away the context and cognitive evaluations of the feelings, and they are pretty much the same core sensations. You can't stop the client from interpreting her urges, thoughts, and emotions about pulling, but if she can become more aware of the process that is taking place, she will be able to see these interpretations for what they are, and accepting their presence will be easier. The following dialogue helps describe this topic.

Case Vignette

Therapist: We are going to do another sort of goofy exercise. When we usually describe something, we use its physical properties as well as our evaluations of it. For example, the physical properties of this pen are that it is blue, plastic, hard, skinny, smooth, etc. And my evaluations of it are that it is useful and the appropriate color for business, it was inexpensive, or perhaps my wife gave it to me and it has emotional meaning. If every person on the planet disappeared and an alien found this pen in 1,000 years the properties of blue, plastic, hard, skinny, and smooth would still exist, but the alien would not say it is appropriate or meaningful—those are properties that are not in the object. Properties such as those are verbal—they are not real. Let's look at your urges to pull hair. What are the properties of your urges that nobody would argue with?

Client: I can sense a tingle in the area where I pull from. I have tension throughout my body. It is uncomfortable.

Therapist: Is being uncomfortable actually part of the urge? Isn't that something that was added?

Client: Yeah, I guess so.

Therapist: Good. Now let's look at some of the properties of the urge that are added; they are your evaluations of it.

Client: It is bad; it is uncomfortable; it hurts sometimes, etc.

Therapist: Great. Do you see the difference between the two? If I paid you a million dollars for every minute you felt the urge, it would no longer be bad or uncomfortable, but it would still be tingly and make your body tense. Even for one million dollars you could not change its properties. Keep this in mind next time you are struggling with this urge. There are parts of the urge that are real and parts of it that are added by your mind.

Exercise—The Pull of Your Mind

As written earlier, clients often come into therapy with the belief that the therapist will be able to stop or lessen their urges to pull. The focus of ACT is to help the client function better in the presence of these feelings, while not trying to control them. This concept is important because the more the client thinks she should not have urges, thoughts, or emotions that lead to pulling, the more likely it is that she will end up in a struggle with them. One nice way to help a client see this is through the "pull of your mind exercise." This will help the client experience that one thought will always pull another. Often what happens is that the opposite thought is pulled. Thus, the more the client struggles to control her urges, the stronger they will be. We do this exercise with TTM-related thoughts rather than general thoughts because it increases their emotional content. The exercise involves stating a thought that has to do with hair pulling and helping the client see how it pulls her thoughts in the other direction. First give the client the following instructions:

I am going to say a couple statements that have to do with your hair pulling. I want you to see what your mind does with them. Most people say that their mind does something with them; they respond to the statements in some way. Close your eyes and tell me what your mind says after I say the following thoughts. There is no need to say more, just tell me what your mind says first.

■ *There is nothing wrong with pulling.*

■ *There are no good qualities to pulling.*

- *Only people who are messed up pull hair.*

- *Stopping hair pulling is easy.*

- *You can control your urges to pull.*

- *You can't control your urges to pull.*

Say a number of bold statements and see how the client responds to them. It is likely that clients will say the opposite of the statement. For example, if you said *there is nothing wrong with pulling,* or *there are no good qualities to pulling,* they are opposite statements, but neither is totally true. The client's mind will find the opposite of these statements. Help the client see this. Finally, through discussion, help the client see that trying to talk herself out of the thoughts she has while pulling will ultimately pull her into the struggle with her pulling, rather than take her out if it. The mind is too smart for this—it will automatically pull in the opposite direction.

Exercise—Take Your Urges with You

Have the client write her main thought about hair pulling on a 3 x 5 card and carry it with her every day. She can put it in her purse or tape it to the mirror so she sees it every day. The purpose of this exercise is to help the client see her urges to pull or pulling-related thoughts in a different way. In the pulling moment they are felt as *bad and dangerous,* but outside of that moment they are just thoughts.

Exercise—Talking for the Client

This exercise should only be done with clients who are less defensive and more willing to have some difficult emotions. This is a good exercise for a client who is doing well in therapy and on board with the ACT approach to TTM. It is a typical defusion exercise in which the client has the opportunity to see her urges to pull hair in a different way.

Have the client get in a position where she is ready to start pulling. We usually have the client look in a mirror at the area that she pulls from.

Having her hold one of her usual pulling tools can also help the exercise. Instead of having the client talk about her thoughts about hair pulling, you will do the thinking for her. Say aloud what you believe the client is thinking. Then, switch roles and have the client speak for you. This exercise can be described in the following way:

> *We are going to do another exercise where you get to see your thoughts about pulling in a different way. I want you to get in a position where your thoughts about pulling would show up. In order to see them in a different way, I am going to talk for them. I am going to be your mind for a little bit. I am not making fun of you or picking on your thoughts. I just want you to be able to see them in a different light. If you start talking back to your mind, I will have to tell you it is not your turn.*

After doing this for a few minutes, let the client speak for you. Pretend you are about to start pulling (e.g., look in a mirror and hold a pair of tweezers). The thoughts verbalized by the client are likely the very same thoughts she has herself. Continue this exercise for another couple minutes.

Once the exercise has been completed, discuss with the client her reactions to the practice. Although most clients report that this is a funny exercise, it is a very effective way of helping clients view their thoughts about pulling in a less literal way.

Homework

- Instruct the client to engage in the Being Present exercise for 10 minutes every day until the next session

- The client should continue to monitor hair-pulling episodes over the course of the next week using the TTM Self-Monitoring Form, engage in the chosen competing response, and implement stimulus control procedures

- The client and therapist should agree to engage in a new behavioral commitment exercise and should continue the previous ones.

Chapter 9 | *Session 8: Practicing Acceptance and Commitment Therapy (ACT)*

(Corresponds to chapter 7 of the workbook)

Materials Needed

- Making Friends with Your Urges form

Session Outline

- Conduct weekly assessment of progress

- Inquire about any reactions to material from previous session

- Review homework

- Discuss acceptance and defusion as learned skills that require practice

- Assign homework

Completion of Assessment Measures

As in every session, the client should return or complete an assessment to gauge progress. This progress (or lack of it) and the client's reactions should be discussed. Help the client plot assessment data on the graph provided in the workbook.

Review of Previous Material

Ask the client to share her thoughts on and reactions to the topics discussed in Sessions 6 and 7.

Homework Review

Praise the client for engaging in the self-monitoring process. Review and troubleshoot implementation of the HRT and stimulus control procedures. Point out the importance of continued monitoring and use of competing responses and stimulus control procedures. Plot the self-monitoring data on the daily graph (in the workbook) to examine fluctuations in pulling. Discuss patterns and trends in the data, and ask the client why she thinks certain trends in the pulling may have developed. Give the client the opportunity to acknowledge any reactions she may have had to pulling-related private experiences. Review results of behavioral commitment exercises in Sessions 6 and 7.

Embracing the Urge

At this point, the client should be aware that urges to pull are incredibly difficult to control, that attempts to control them are often more of a problem than the urges themselves, and that the private experiences surrounding pulling present themselves as much more real and literal than they really are. Therefore, learning to accept their presence in life might be a more functional way to address them. This session, and the session that follows, gives the client some opportunities to work with this new ACT way of looking at her hair pulling. Behavior therapists and other therapists who work with anxiety disorders will be quite familiar with this type of work. We suggest using procedures from exposure therapy and doing so in a context where the client is encouraged to "make friends" with the urge to pull and to see these experiences for what they really are—just feelings, sensations, and words in her head. In this sense, the exposure is not done to reduce unpleasant experiences. Such a reduction might occur because of natural habituation and extinction processes, but that is not the goal of this work. "Exposure" in this program is considered successful if the client is willing to accept the urge without fighting it, not if there is a reduction in the occurrence of urges.

Some of this type of work has occurred in previous behavioral commitment exercises, but these have slightly different functions. The previous exercises were more about following the client's values; the exercises presented here are more about practicing the skills that have been taught in session. There is certainly a lot of overlap, but these in-session exercises are more like practicing skills than real-life situations. To use an analogy, behavioral commitments are like the race and these are like the practices. Practices are always a lot longer and harder than the actual race.

Case Vignette

Therapist: Up until you started working with me, you put quite a lot of effort into controlling your urges to pull hair, and, interestingly, that did not work out that well. There was a lot of time spent controlling the uncontrollable, and you never really stopped pulling. Maybe it is time we started doing the complete opposite of what you have been doing. Instead of working to control these feelings, like you had been doing, let's practice making room for them. What do you do that brings on your urges to hair pull?

Client: Mirrors, tweezers, and touching my hair.

Therapist: OK, let's use the items on that list and purposefully work with them. We are not taking them out to pull; we are taking them out to make friends with your urges to pull.

Client: So what do you want me to do?

Therapist: If you are willing, we will work on getting your urge to pull to show up so that we can practice functioning with it. We're going to use some of the things that trigger your urge, and play with them a little. This is like playing Game 2 while the player in Game 1 taunts you and tries to get you to play her game. The rules for this exercise are as follows: pick a specific behavior, do it for a specific amount of time, while being open to what shows up and noticing it for what it really is. It does not have to do with how much the other team taunts you. I would like you to participate in the exercise until your time is up. The exercise has nothing to do with getting used to the urge or decreasing it. I just want you to become familiar with it. Know it fully. Don't run away from it. The longer you stay around something, the more you get to know it.

Work with the client to pick a specific behavior such as looking in a mirror for 10 minutes, holding a tweezers for 10 minutes, or pulling out one hair to get the urge to show up. There should be an agreement to engage in the exercise for a specific amount of time. This exercise is different from exposure that is done with anxiety disorders in that there is no concern about the strength of the urge or thoughts about pulling. It does not matter how high or low the urge or thoughts are, or if they decrease throughout the session. The focus is on how open the client is to what is there. If the client notes that the urge is decreasing, ask, *"Is that what we are about here?"* The client needs to be reoriented to increasing her acceptance of the urge, defusing the literal meaning of the urge, remembering the values she is working toward, and committing to behavior change and succeeding with it.

This exercise also provides wonderful opportunities for the therapist to strengthen the processes that have already been targeted: acceptance, defusion, and values. These processes are a little more difficult to detect if you are less familiar with ACT. But generally, if the client is unwilling to experience any part of the urge to pull hair, then acceptance may be targeted. If the client experiences the urge to pull as a real and dangerous thing, then more defusion processes can be targeted. Also, if the client lacks motivation or is not fully invested in the exposure, then a discussion of values can be useful.

Following are examples of occurrence of one of these processes and possible responses to them.

Acceptance

Avoidance can generally be detected when a client refuses or avoids a feeling, thought, or private event. This might occur in this exercise when a client is not willing to do a part of it or suggests doing something easier.

Ways to address avoidance in session:

- Ask the client if they are playing Game 1 or Game 2.
- Ask the client to "open up" a little to the feeling she is pushing away.

Defusion

The process of defusion needs to be addressed when the client appears to be pushed around by her thoughts about pulling and her urges to pull. You can generally detect that these events are being taken literally when the client appears fearful of them—as though they are real things. The client might say something like, "But won't that make it so bad that I end up pulling?" Fusion is generally addressed by helping the client see that thoughts, feelings, and bodily sensations are not real things to fight with.

Ways to address fusion:

- Ask the client if the private event is real, like the table or some other real object in the room.

- Say "thank your mind for that thought" or "that is an interesting one."

- Use silly descriptions of the private events established in Sessions 6 and 7.

Values

If the client is not willing to participate in the exercise, then it is usually a good idea to link the exercise to something that is important to the client. Exposing the client to her urges to pull is not an end in itself, but is done in the service of something meaningful, like being with her family more or just having a full head of hair. Simply linking the exercise to these activities should increase motivation to participate in the exercise.

Ways to address lack of motivation to participate:

- Ask the client why she is in therapy and what she has to gain from learning to function with her urges.

- Say "this exercise might bring you one step closer to [insert client's valued activity]."

Homework

✎ Ask the client to complete the Making Friends with Your Urges form in the workbook as a way to identify those situations where the urges and other private events surrounding pulling are likely to occur.

✎ The client should continue to monitor hair-pulling episodes over the course of the next week using the TTM Self-Monitoring Form, engage in the chosen competing response, and implement stimulus control procedures. Fade out from everyday use those stimulus control procedures the client has been addressing in the Session 8 and 9 Embracing Your Urges exercises.

✎ The client and therapist should agree to engage in a new behavioral commitment exercise and should continue the previous ones.

Chapter 10 | *Session 9: Practicing ACT and Review*

(Corresponds to chapter 8 of the workbook)

There are no materials needed for this session.

Session Outline

- Conduct weekly assessment of progress

- Inquire about any reactions to material from previous session

- Review homework

- Continue Embracing the Urge exercises conducted last week

- Introduce relapse prevention

- Assign homework

Completion of Assessment Measures

As in every session, the client should return or complete an assessment to gauge progress. This progress (or lack of it) and the client's reactions should be discussed. Help the client plot assessment data on the graph provided in the workbook.

Review of Previous Material

Ask the client to share her thoughts on and reactions to the topics discussed in the previous session.

Homework Review

Praise the client for engaging in the self-monitoring and using HRT and stimulus control procedures, and point out the importance of continued monitoring and use of competing responses and stimulus control exercises. Plot the self-monitoring data on the daily graph (in the workbook) to examine fluctuations in pulling. Discuss patterns and trends in the data, and give the client the opportunity to acknowledge any reactions she may have had to use of the HRT procedures and pulling-related private experiences. Any difficulties the client had should be addressed, and any necessary modifications to the procedure should be made. Review results of behavioral commitment exercises in Session 8. Review the client's completed Making Friends with Your Urges form and discuss her success in accepting her private experiences.

Continue with Embracing the Urge Exercises

Continue with exposure to pulling cues done in Session 8. Again, the focus of this practice should be on providing the client with an opportunity to practice ACT skills, not on reduction of the private experience.

Relapse Prevention: Reviewing What's Been Learned

Ask the client to review the therapy and tell you what she has learned. Make contact with the following points.

- There are two different types of pulling: focused and non-focused, or automatic pulling.

- Habit reversal is used to control pulling, and ACT procedures are used to step out of the struggle with urges and other private experiences.

- Review the benefits of moving in the direction of values instead of focusing energy on controlling a feeling.

- Urges can't be controlled.

- It is the attempt to control the urge that is the problem and not the urge itself.

- Another option for trying to control the urge is to make room for the urge in your life, through acceptance. Habit reversal can help you allow the urge to be present and, in that way, can facilitate acceptance.

- Your urge is not a real thing that you have to fight with.

- We work hard to make room for the urge and gain control over pulling because there is something important in doing so to you, not because you have to.

- These skills require consistent practice in our lives.

Homework

✎ Ask the client to identify other barriers to maintaining treatment gains.

✎ The client should continue to monitor hair-pulling episodes using the TTM Self Monitoring Form over the course of the next week, engage in the chosen competing response, and implement stimulus control procedures.

✎ Instruct the client to continue behavioral commitment exercises while using HRT procedures and practicing acceptance and defusion.

Chapter 11 | *Session 10: Review and Relapse Prevention*

(Corresponds to chapter 9 of the workbook)

There are no materials needed for this session.

Session Outline

- Conduct weekly assessment of progress

- Inquire about any reactions to material from previous session

- Review homework

- Discuss relapse prevention techniques

- Celebrate accomplishments and completion of therapy

Completion of Assessment Measures

Today the client will complete her final weekly assessment. Using her previously completed assessments, point out the progress the client has made in treatment. Plot the latest data on the graph of progress.

Review of Previous Material

Ask the client to share her thoughts on and reactions to the topics discussed in the previous session. This is the client's last chance to clarify concepts and ask any questions she may have.

Homework Review

Praise the client for engaging in the self-monitoring and using HRT and stimulus control procedures, and point out the importance of continued monitoring and use of competing responses and stimulus control procedures. Plot the self-monitoring data on the daily graph (in the workbook) to examine fluctuations in pulling. Discuss patterns and trends in the data, and give the client the opportunity to acknowledge any reactions she may have had to use of the HRT procedures and pulling-related private experiences. Review results of behavioral commitment exercises in Session 9, paying particular attention to the application of defusion exercises.

Review of Relapse Prevention Strategies

Remind the client to continue using the skills learned in therapy, and discuss common pitfalls and methods for addressing them. The two main pitfalls are 1) letting pulling return and 2) falling back into Game 1. Falling back into Game 1 will result in more time fighting with urges, increased pulling, and less time pursuing the meaningful parts of life. Remind the client to start using the HRT procedures if she notices that some of her pulling starts occurring. In addition, encourage the client to look back over her workbook and remind herself of the work that was done, especially in high-risk situations (e.g., life crises, stressful days). It can be easy to fall back into old patterns of emotional control because they are so well supported in society. It was only in therapy where emotional control was not encouraged. The client must work to bring that with her or help it resurface.

Lapse versus Relapse

Discuss with the client the possibility that there may be occasions when her pulling starts to increase and she is spending less time working on controlling it. Frame this possibility as a lapse, rather than a complete relapse. A *lapse* is a slip or partial loss of improvement. Lapses may occur during stressful situations or personal problems or may simply be due to lack of practice of the skills learned in treatment. If the client experiences a lapse, encourage her to look at it as an opportunity to reevaluate how she is responding to her urges to pull and efforts to use HRT procedures.

Vigilance in Using HRT

The client should be made aware of typical patterns in HRT compliance. As persons using HRT begin to have success, they typically become less compliant with the procedure. To counter this, it may be useful for the client to schedule daily practice sessions during which she practices the HRT procedures on simulated hair-pulling episodes.

Increase in Cognitive Fusion

Because the client is functioning in a daily context that supports cognitive fusion, she may find herself reacting to pulling-related thoughts, urges, or emotions as if they were real events with physical characteristics. If the client notices this, establish a plan in which the client reminds herself of the defusion exercises and practices them on a daily basis.

Returning to the Old Agenda

The client may begin to notice a return to an old agenda of attempting to control negative private experiences. An increase in pulling may be a signal that this is occurring. Should the client notice that this is occurring, she should call the therapist and discuss possible ways to return to the agenda of acceptance and willingness.

Celebrating the Completion of Therapy

In this phase, review with the client the progress made in therapy. Congratulate the client on her progress. Answer any questions about future issues or her options for booster sessions, and terminate the session.

Appendix A *Assessment Measures*

The Milwaukee Inventory for Styles of Trichotillomania–Adult Report

Please choose a number which best represents how the question fits your hair-pulling behavior.

0 —— 1 —— 2 —— 3 —— 4 —— 5 —— 6 —— 7 —— 8 —— 9

not true
for any of my
pulling

true for about
half of my pulling

true for
all of my
pulling

1. I pull my hair when I am concentrating on another activity. _____

2. I pull my hair when I am thinking about something unrelated to hair pulling. _____

3. I am in an almost "trance-like" state when I pull my hair. _____

4. I have thoughts about wanting to pull my hair before I actually pull. _____

5. I use tweezers or some other device other than my fingers to pull my hair. _____

6. I pull my hair while I am looking in the mirror. _____

7. I am usually not aware of pulling my hair during a pulling episode. _____

8. I pull my hair when I am anxious or upset. _____

9. I intentionally start pulling my hair. _____

10. I pull my hair when I am experiencing a negative emotion, such as stress, _____
    anger, frustration, or sadness.

11. I have a "strange" sensation just before I pull my hair. _____

12. I don't notice that I have pulled my hair until after it's happened. _____

13. I pull my hair because of something that has happened to me during the day. _____

14. I pull my hair to get rid of an unpleasant urge, feeling, or thought. _____

15. I pull my hair to control how I feel. _____

MIST-A-Scoring Template

The MIST-A contains two distinct scales. Scale 1 is referred to as the Focused Pulling Scale and includes items 4–6, 8–11, and 13–15, while the Automatic Pulling Scale includes items 1–3, 7, and 12. Scoring is relatively straightforward. Simply add the client's scores for each item on these respective scales to yield a total scale score. Higher scores indicate increasingly focused and/or automatic pulling, respectively. Flessner, Woods, Franklin, Cashin, and Keuthen (in press) reported means and standard deviations for the Focused ($M = 45.4$, $SD = 16.2$) and Automatic ($M = 25.7$, $SD = 9.04$) scales based on data obtained from an Internet sample of participants reporting symptoms of TTM (e.g., chronic hair pulling).

Source: Flessner, C. A., Woods, D. W., Franklin, M. E., Cashin, S. E., Keuthen, N. J., & Trichotillomania Learning Center Scientific Advisory Board. (in press). The Milwaukee Inventory for Subtypes of Trichotillomania-Adults (MIST-A): Development, exploratory factor analysis, and psychometric properties. *Journal of Psychopathology and Behavioral Assessment.*

Acceptance and Action Questionnaire (AAQ)

Below you will find a list of statements. Please rate the truth of each statement as it applies to you. Use the following scale to make your choice.

1 ——— 2 ——— 3 ——— 4 ——— 5 ——— 6 ——— 7

| never true | very seldom true | seldom true | sometimes true | frequently true | almost always true | always true |

_____ 1. I am able to take action on a problem even if I am uncertain what the right thing to do is.

_____ 2. I often catch myself daydreaming about things I've done and what I would do differently next time.

_____ 3. When I feel depressed or anxious, I am unable to take care of my responsibilities.

_____ 4. I rarely worry about getting my anxieties, worries, and feelings under control.

_____ 5. I'm not afraid of my feelings.

_____ 6. When I evaluate something negatively, I usually recognize that this is just a reaction, not an objective fact.

_____ 7. When I compare myself to other people, it seems that most of them are handling their lives better than I do.

_____ 8. Anxiety is bad.

_____ 9. If I could magically remove all the painful experiences I've had in my life, I would do so.

Reprinted with permission. Hayes, S. C., Strosahl, K. D., Wilson, K. G., Bissett, R. T., Pistorello, J., Toarmino, D., Polusny, M., A., Dykstra, T. A., Batten, S. V., Bergan, J., Stewart, S. H., Zvolensky, M. J., Eifert, G. H., Bond, F. W., Forsyth J. P., Karekla, M., & McCurry, S. M. (2004). Measuring experiential avoidance: A preliminary test of a working model. _The Psychological Record, 54_, 553–578.

Acceptance and Action Questionnaire for Trichotillomania (AAQ-4TTM)

Below you will find a list of statements. Please rate the truth of each statement as it applies to you. Use the following scale to make your choice.

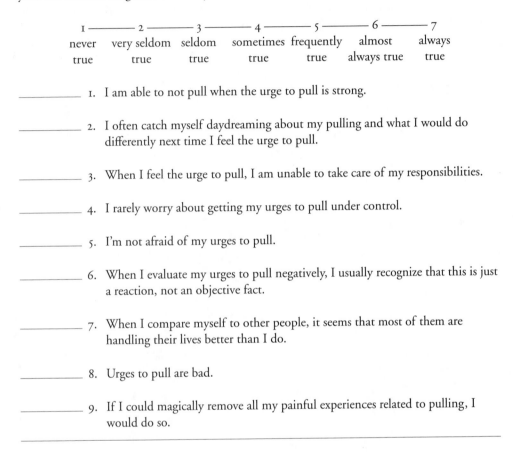

1 ———— 2 ———— 3 ———— 4 ———— 5 ———— 6 ———— 7
never   very seldom   seldom   sometimes   frequently   almost   always
true   true   true   true   true   always true   true

_____ 1. I am able to not pull when the urge to pull is strong.

_____ 2. I often catch myself daydreaming about my pulling and what I would do differently next time I feel the urge to pull.

_____ 3. When I feel the urge to pull, I am unable to take care of my responsibilities.

_____ 4. I rarely worry about getting my urges to pull under control.

_____ 5. I'm not afraid of my urges to pull.

_____ 6. When I evaluate my urges to pull negatively, I usually recognize that this is just a reaction, not an objective fact.

_____ 7. When I compare myself to other people, it seems that most of them are handling their lives better than I do.

_____ 8. Urges to pull are bad.

_____ 9. If I could magically remove all my painful experiences related to pulling, I would do so.

Scoring Template for AAQ and AAQ-4TTM

The AAQ has a maximum score of 63 and a minimum score of 7. Lower scores indicate less cognitive fusion, emotional avoidance, and behavioral inaction, and greater defusion, acceptance, and behavioral commitment. Before scoring, reverse items 1, 4, 5, and 6, and then sum the scores. The mean scores for the AAQ in a clinical sample were 37.3 for females and 34.7 for males, whereas the mean scores in a nonclinical sample were 33.4 for females and 33.2 for males. The AAQ-4TTM is scored in the same way as the original AAQ. However, normative data for the AAQ-4TTM do not exist.

Appendix B *Forms and Handouts*

What Is Trichotillomania?

Trichotillomania, or TTM, is chronic hair pulling resulting in noticeable hair loss. Individuals usually feel an increasing sense of tension immediately prior to pulling out the hair or when attempting to resist pulling and feel a sense of gratification when pulling hair. Individuals typically experience significant distress or impairment in important areas of their life due to their struggles with the urges to pull and the hair pulling itself.

The places people most commonly pull hair from are as follows:

- Scalp
- Eyebrows
- Eyelashes
- Beards
- Pubic hair

Prevalence

Research estimates are limited, however, it is speculated that somewhere between 10% and 15% of young adults pull hair, but only 2% to 3% experiencing noticeable loss and significant distress from pulling. Thus, hair pulling may occur on a continuum, ranging from benign hair pulling to more severe pulling that results in noticeable hair loss and distress.

Gender Differences

Many more adult women present for trichotillomania treatment than men. This difference may only account for the number of people seeking help rather than actual differences in rates of trichotillomania. For example, in children the gender distribution may be closer to equal.

Associated Problems

People with TTM often experience anxiety and depression, and may engage in other habitual behaviors such as skin picking, nail biting, or thumb and finger sucking.

Age of Onset

Mean age of onset is approximately 13 years. Hair pulling is sometimes preceded by a stressful life event or a change in environmental conditions, but in many cases there is no clear reason for it beginning.

Patterns of Hair Pulling

Sometimes touching or stroking of the hairs occurs before pulling. Hair pulling is usually done by wrapping strands around the index finger when hair is long or by grasping shorter hair by the thumb and index finger. Others may use tweezers to help them pull. Most often, hair is pulled from one's own body, but some individuals report pulling from other people or even their pets.

After hair is pulled, it may be discarded or used for post-pulling rituals. Many people report rubbing pulled hair between their index finger and thumb. Others chew or bite on the pulled hair.

Genetic and Biological Factors

There is an increased probability of hair pulling, along with other psychiatric disorders, in first-degree relatives of individuals diagnosed with trichotillomania. The most common associated diagnoses found in first-degree relatives are depressive disorder, anxiety disorder, and substance abuse. Individuals with trichotillomania may have a higher threshold for pain, however, data are inconclusive.

Automatic and Focused Hair Pulling

Automatic hair pulling is when you pull outside of awareness, while absorbed in an activity that requires your attention. Often you don't know you are pulling until you are well into an episode or have already finished. About 75% of pulling falls into this category.

Focused pulling describes pulling with awareness, and a strong urge to engage in pulling. Individuals who report focused pulling typically also report reductions in anxiety or tension after pulling. This type of pulling is done to control private experiences such as urges, sensations, thoughts, or emotions.

Completion Instructions for Stimulus Control Assessment Form (SCAF)

General Instructions:

The SCAF should be completed in Session 1 of AEBT-T. The SCAF should be completed by the therapist in conjunction with the client.

Specific Administration Instructions:

1. In the "Pulling Site" column of the SCAF, the therapist writes down a recognizable description of all bodily sites from which the client pulls. The order in which sites are written is not important.

2. Before completing the SCAF, the therapist should deliver the following instructions to the client (italicized text represents what the therapist should read to the client):

    We are going to spend some time trying to determine when your pulling is more likely to happen. We're going to go through each bodily site from which you pull.

3. For each pulling site, the therapist will ask the following questions:

    I'm going to first ask you about your [describe specific pulling site].

    I'm going to ask you about settings in which you may pull, instruments you may use to help you pull, and whether other people are around when you pull. Please say "yes," if [pulling site] *is more likely to occur at this time or in this situation.*

If the description is sufficiently different from what has already been checked, write down a description of the antecedent in one of the "other" boxes, and check the corresponding box. Ask for as much detail about each situation as you can, and take notes in the corresponding box. Continue with this process until the client has exhausted all antecedents for the pulling currently being discussed.

Pulling Site	Settings						Tools Used				Social Presence
	Bedroom	Watching TV or Playing Video Games	Reading	Bathroom	Other	Other	Tweezers	Needles, Safety Pins, Sharp Objects	Mirrors, Reflective Objects	Other	Others Present When Pulling

References

American Psychiatric Association. *Diagnostic and statistical manual of mental disorders* (4th ed., Text Revision). Washington, DC: American Psychiatric Press, 2000.

Antony, M. M., Bieling, P. J., Cox, B. J., Enns, M. W., & Swinson, R. P. (1998). Psychometric properties of the 42-item and 21-item versions of the Depression Anxiety Stress Scales in clinical groups and a community sample. *Psychological Assessment, 10,* 176–181.

Begotka, A. M., Woods, D. W., & Wetterneck, C. T. (2003, November). The Relationship Between Experiential Avoidance and the Severity of Trichotillomania in a Nonreferred Sample. In M. E. Franklin & N. J. Keuthen (Chairs), *New Developments in Trichotillomania Research.* Symposium conducted at the meeting of the Association for the Advancement of Behavior Therapy, Boston, MA.

Begotka, A. M., Woods, D. W., & Wetterneck, C. T. (2004). The relationship between experiential avoidance and the severity of trichotillomania in a nonreferred sample. *Journal of Behavior Therapy and Experimental Psychiatry, 35,* 17–24.

Christenson, G. A., & Mackenzie, T. B. (1994). Trichotillomania. In M. Hersen & R. T. Ammerman (Eds.), *Handbook of prescriptive treatment for adults* (pp. 217–235). New York: Plenum Press.

Christenson, G. A., Mackenzie, T. B., & Mitchell, J. E. (1991). Characteristics of 60 adult chronic hair pullers. *American Journal of Psychiatry, 148,* 365–370.

Christenson, G. A., Mackenzie, T. B., & Mitchell, J. E. (1994). Adult men and women with trichotillomania. A comparison of male and female characteristics. *Psychosomatics, 135,* 142–149.

Christenson, G. A., & Mansueto, C. S. (1999). Trichotillomania: Descriptive characteristics and phenomenology. In D. J. Stein, G. A. Christenson, & E. Hollander (Eds.). *Trichotillomania* (pp. 1–42). Washington, DC: American Psychiatric Press.

Christenson, G. A., Pyle, R. L., & Mitchell J. E. (1991). Estimated lifetime prevalence of trichotillomania in college students. *Journal of Clinical Psychiatry, 52,* 415–417.

Diefenbach, G. J., Mouton-Odum, S., & Stanley, M. A. (2002). Affective correlates of trichotillomania. *Behaviour Research and Therapy, 40,* 1305–1315.

du Toit, P. L., van Kradenburg, J., Niehaus, D. J. H., & Stein, D. J. (2001). Characteristics and phenomenology of hair-pulling: An exploration of subtypes. *Comprehensive Psychiatry, 42,* 247–256.

Flessner, C. A., Woods, D. W., Franklin, M. E., Cashin, S. E., Keuthen, N. J., & the Trichotillomania Learning Center Scientific Advisory Board. (In Press). The Milwaukee Inventory of Subtypes of Trichotillomania–Adult (MIST-A): Development of an instrument for the assessment of "focused" and "automatic" hair pulling in adults. *Journal of Psychopathology and Behavioral Assessment.*

Grant, J. E., Odlaug, B. L., & Potenza, M. N. (2007). Addicted to hair pulling? How an alternate model of trichotillomania may improve treatment outcome. *Harvard Review of Psychiatry, 15,* 80–85.

Hayes, S. C., Barnes-Holmes, D., & Roche, B. (Eds.). (2001). *Relational frame theory: A post-Skinnerian account of human language and cognition.* New York: Kluwer Academic/Plenum Publishers.

Hayes, S. C., Bissett, R. T., Strosahl, K., Wilson, K., Pistorello, J., Toarmina, M., Polusny, M. A., Batten, S. V., Dykstra, T. A., Stewart, S. H., Zvolensky, M. J., Eifert, G. H., Bergan, J., & Follette, W. C. (2004). Measuring experiential avoidance: A preliminary test of a working model. *The Psychological Record, 54,* 553–578.

Hayes, S. C., Strosahl, K. D., & Wilson, K. G. (1999). *Acceptance and Commitment Therapy: An Experiential Approach to Behavior Change.* New York: Guilford Press.

Hayes, S. C., Wilson, K. G., Gifford, E. V., Follette, V. M., & Strosahl, K. (1996). Experiential avoidance and behavioral disorders: A functional dimensional approach to diagnosis and treatment. *Journal of Consulting and Clinical Psychology, 64,* 1152–1168.

Keuthen, N. J., Flessner, C. A., Woods, D. W., Franklin, M. E., Stein, D. J., & TLC-SAB. (2007). Factor Analysis of the Massachusetts General Hospital Hairpulling Scale, *Journal of Psychosomatic Research, 62,* 702–709.

Keuthen, N. J., Franklin, M. E., Bohne, A., Bromley, M., Levy, J., Jenike, M. A., & Neziroglu, F. (2002). Functional impairments associated with trichotillomania and implications for treatment development. In N. J. Keuthen (Chair), *Trichotillomania: Psychopathology and Treatment De-*

velopment. Symposium conducted at the annual meeting of the Association for the Advancement of Behavior Therapy, Reno, NV.

Keuthen, N. J., O'Sullivan, R. L., Ricciardi, J. N., Shera, D., Savage, C. A., Borgmann, A. S., Jenike, M. A., & Baer, L. (1995). The Massachusetts General Hospital (MGH) Hairpulling Scale: 1. Development and factor analysis. *Psychotherapy and Psychosomatics, 64,* 141–145.

Keuthen, N. J., Stein, D. J., & Christenson, G. A. (2001). *Help for hairpullers: Understanding and coping with trichotillomania.* Oakland, CA: New Harbinger Publications.

Lovibond, S. H., & Lovibond, P. F. (1995). *Manual for the Depression and Anxiety Stress Scales* (second ed.). Sydney, Australia: Psychological Foundation of Australia.

Mackenzie, T. B., Ristvedt, S. L., Christenson, G. A., Smith Lebow, A., & Mitchell, J. E. (1995). Identification of cues associated with compulsive, bulimic, and hair-pulling symptoms. *Journal of Behavior Therapy and Experimental Psychiatry, 26,* 9–16.

Mansueto, C. S., Townsley-Stemberger, R. M., Thomas, A., & Golomb, R. (1997). Trichotillomania: A comprehensive behavioral model. *Clinical Psychology Review, 17,* 567–577.

Marcks, B. A., Wetterneck, C. T., & Woods, D. W. (2006) Investigating health care providers' knowledge about trichotillomania and its treatment. *Cognitive Behaviour Therapy, 35,* 19–27.

Miltenberger, R. G., Long, E. S., & Rapp, J. T., Lumley, V. A., & Elliott, A. J. (1998). Evaluating the function of hair pulling: A preliminary investigation. *Behavior Therapy, 29,* 211–219.

Ninan, P. T., Rothbaum, B. O., Marsteller, F. A., Knight, B. T., & Eccard, M. B. (2000). A placebo-controlled trial of cognitive-behavioral therapy and clomipramine in trichotillomania. *Journal of Clinical Psychiatry, 61,* 47–50.

Norberg, M. M., Wetterneck, C. T., Woods, D. W., & Conelea C. A. (2007). Experiential avoidance as a mediator of relationships between cognitions and hair-pulling severity. *Behavior Modification, 31(4),* 367–381.

O'Connor, K., Brisebois, H., Brault, M., Robillard, S., & Loiselle, J. (2003). Behavioral activity associated with onset in chronic tic and habit disorder. *Behaviour Research and Therapy, 41(2),* 241–249.

O'Sullivan, R. L., Keuthen, N. J., Hayday, C. F., Ricciardi, J. N., Buttolph, M. L., Jenike, M. A., & Baer, L. (1995). The Massachusetts General Hospital Hairpulling Scale: 2. Reliability and validity. *Psychotherapy and Psychosomatics, 64,* 146–148.

Phillips, M. R., Zaheer, S., & Drugas, G. T. (1998). Gastric trichobezoar: Case report and literature review. *Mayo Clinic Proceedings, 73,* 653–656.

Rapp, J. T., Miltenberger, R. G., Galensky, T. L., Ellingson, S. A., Stricker, J., Garlinghouse, M., & Long, E. S. (2000). Treatment of hair pulling and hair manipulation maintained by digital-tactile stimulation. *Behavior Therapy, 31,* 381–393.

Seedat, S., & Stein, D. J. (1998). Psychosocial and economic implications of trichotillomania: A pilot study in a South African sample. *CNS Spectrums, 3,* 40–43.

Stein, D. J., Christenson, G. A., & Hollander, E. (1999). *Trichotillomania.* Washington, DC: American Psychiatric Press.

Swedo, S. E., Leonard, H. L., Rapoport, J. L., Lenane, M. C., Goldberger, E. L., & Cheslow, D. L. (1989). A double-blind comparison of clomipramine and desipramine in the treatment of trichotillomania (hair pulling). *New England Journal of Medicine, 321,* 497–501.

Twohig, M. P., & Woods, D. W. (2004). A preliminary investigation of acceptance and commitment therapy and habit reversal as a treatment for trichotillomania. *Behavior Therapy, 35,* 803–820.

Van Minnen, A., Hoogduin, K., Keijsers, G., Hellenbrand, I., & Hendriks, G. (2003). Treatment of trichotillomania with behavioral therapy or fluoxetine: A randomized, waiting-list controlled study. *Archives of General Psychiatry, 60,* 517–522.

Wetterneck, C. T., & Woods, D. W. (2005). Hair pulling antecedents in trichotillomania: Their relationship with experiential avoidance. Manuscript submitted for publication.

Wetterneck, C. T., & Woods, D. W. (2007). A contemporary behavior analytic model of trichotillomania. In D. W. Woods & J. Kanter (Eds.), *Understanding Behavior Disorders: A Contemporary Behavioral Perspective* (pp. 157–180). Reno, NV: Context Press.

Wetterneck, C. T., Woods, D. W., Flessner, C. A., Norberg, M., & Begotka, A. (May 2005). *Antecedent Phenomena Associated with Trichotillomania: Research and Treatment Implications for an Online Study.* Symposium presented at the Association for Behavior Analysis conference, Chicago, IL.

Woods, D. W., Flessner, C. A., Franklin, M. E., Keuthen, N. J., Goodwin, R., Stein, D. J., Walther, M., & the Trichotillomania Learning Center Scientific Advisory Board. (2006a). The Trichotillomania Impact Project (TIP): Exploring phenomenology, functional impairment, and treatment utilization. *Journal of Clinical Psychiatry, 67,* 1877–1888.

Woods, D. W., Flessner, C. A., Franklin, M. E., Wetterneck, C. T., Walther, M. R., Anderson, E. R., & Cardona, D. (2006b). Understanding and treating trichotillomania: What we know and what we don't know. *Psychiatric Clinics of North America, 29,* 487–501.

Woods, D. W., & Miltenberger, R. G. (1995). Habit reversal: A review of applications and variations. *Journal of Behavior Therapy and Experimental Psychiatry, 26(2),* 123–131.

Woods, D. W., Wetterneck, C. T., & Flessner, C. A. (2006). A controlled evaluation of acceptance and commitment therapy plus habit reversal for trichotillomania. *Behaviour Research and Therapy, 44,* 639–656.

About the Authors

Douglas W. Woods received his Ph.D. in clinical psychology from Western Michigan University in 1999. He is currently associate professor
of psychology and Director of Clinical Training at the University of Wisconsin-Milwaukee. Dr. Woods is a recognized expert in the assessment and treatment of trichotillomania, Tourette syndrome, and other obsessive-compulsive (OCD) spectrum disorders. Dr. Woods is a member of the Trichotillomania Learning Center's Scientific Advisory Board and the Tourette Syndrome Association's Medical Advisory Board. He has published over 100 journal articles and book chapters on these and related topics, including two books, *Tic Disorders, Trichotillomania, and Other Repetitive Behavior Disorders: A Behavioral Approach to Analysis and Treatment*, and *Treating Tourette Syndrome and Tic Disorders: A Guide for Practitioners*. Dr. Woods' research has been funded by grants from the National Institutes of Health, the Trichotillomania Learning Center, and the Tourette Syndrome Association.

Michael P. Twohig received his Ph.D. from the University of Nevada, Reno, in 2007, and completed his clinical psychology internship at the Anxiety Disorders Clinic at the University of British Columbia. He is currently an assistant professor in the Department of Psychology at Utah State University in Logan, Utah. His research has generally focused on the treatment of OCD and OCD spectrum disorders such as trichotillomania and skin picking. He has authored over 40 scholarly pieces on areas such as OCD and OCD spectrum disorders, habit reversal, and acceptance and commitment therapy (ACT). He is author of *ACT Verbatim for Depression and Anxiety: Annotated Transcripts for Learning Acceptance and Commitment Therapy* with Steven C. Hayes, Ph.D. His work on the application of ACT to OCD and OCD spectrum disorders has been funded by the National Institute of Health (with Steven Hayes) and the Trichotillomania Learning Center (with Douglas W. Woods).